KU-758-505

POCKET
FINANCE

OTHER TITLES FROM
THE ECONOMIST BOOKS

The Economist Desk Companion
The Economist Guide to Analysing Companies
The Economist Guide to Economic Indicators
The Economist Guide to the European Union
The Economist Numbers Guide
The Economist Style Guide
Going Digital
The International Dictionary of Finance
Pocket Accounting
Pocket Director
Pocket Employer
Pocket Information Technology
Pocket Investor
Pocket Law
Pocket Manager
Pocket Marketing
Pocket MBA
Pocket Negotiator
Pocket Strategy
Pocket Telecommunications
The Economist Pocket Africa
The Economist Pocket Asia
The Economist Pocket Britain in Figures
The Economist Pocket Europe in Figures
The Economist Pocket Latin America
The Economist Pocket Middle East
The Economist Pocket USA
The Economist Pocket World in Figures

POCKET
FINANCE

TIM HINDLE

THE ECONOMIST IN ASSOCIATION WITH
PROFILE BOOKS LTD

Profile Books Ltd, Registered Office:
62 Queen Anne Street, London W1M 9LA

This edition published by Profile Books Ltd
in association with
The Economist Newspaper Ltd 1997

Copyright © The Economist Newspaper Ltd, 1994, 1997

All rights reserved. Without limiting the rights under copyright
reserved above, no part of this publication may be reproduced,
stored in or introduced into a retrieval system, or transmitted, in
any form or by any means (electronic, mechanical, photocopying,
recording or otherwise), without the prior written permission of
both the copyright owner and the publisher of this book.

The greatest care has been taken in compiling this book. However,
no responsibility can be accepted by the publishers or compilers
for the accuracy of the information presented.
Where opinion is expressed it is that of the author and does not
necessarily coincide with the editorial views of
The Economist Newspaper.

Printed by
LEGO S.p.a. - Vicenza - Italy

A CIP catalogue record for this book is available
from the British Library

ISBN 1 86197 017 X

CONTENTS

INTRODUCTION

Pocket Finance is one in a series of books that brings the clarity for which *The Economist* is famous to the often confusing subject of business. It is written by Tim Hindle, a former finance editor of *The Economist*, and is divided into three parts.

Part 1 consists of essays which look at several of the most important features and issues concerning the way the financial world operates today.

Part 2 is an A–Z of terms which are widely used by those in finance and business but not always fully understood by those using them. Throughout this section are sprinkled lively quotations providing often witty insights, together with numerous nuggets of fact, many highlighting notable financial ups and downs.

In this section words in small capitals usually indicate a separate entry, thus enabling readers to find other relevant information (though they should note that abbreviations, such as EU and IBM, are also in small capitals).

Part 3 consists of numerous appendixes with information in the form of tabulated data, providing easy reference to a great variety of financial subjects. The Pocket Management series is designed to take the mystique out of business and financial jargon in a stimulating and entertaining way.

Other titles in the series are:

Pocket Accounting
Pocket Director
Pocket Employer
Pocket Information Technology
Pocket Investor
Pocket Law
Pocket Manager
Pocket Marketing
Pocket MBA
Pocket Negotiator
Pocket Strategy
Pocket Telecommunications

Part 1

ESSAYS

TRACKING SAVINGS FROM THEIR SOURCE

Money, of course, makes the world go round. Nevertheless it is surprising that the allocation of it to different competing demands should occupy so many waking hours of some of the greatest minds on the planet. In the USA, Europe and Japan the brightest and most worldly young graduates are attracted by the idea of working in financial markets. There they find problem-solving galore (the staple diet of their business education); the prospect of ample foreign travel; like-minded workmates; and a salary that will never be mean, and may even be handsome.

In all this, however, they should not lose sight of the fact that finance and financial markets are only a means to an end. Bankers, stockbrokers and the like are merely conduits that pass money from an original saver to a final user. The conduits often try to make themselves seem more important than either the saver or the borrower, using devices like posh accents, dark suits and tall glass buildings to achieve their desired effect. But the truth is that only a few generations ago bankers were no more than moneylenders, and financial markets no more significant than a fish or a fur bazaar.

In the beginning

All finance begins with saving, that is, somebody's decision to consume less now in order to be able to consume more later. In this sense financial institutions are to money what the video-cassette recorder is to broadcasting: they enable consumers to time-shift their consumption.

Financial institutions bridge the gap between the time when people decide to save and the time when they decide to consume. Modern developed societies tend to save around 15–20% of their GNP, the total value of what they produce during the year. In other words, out of every $10 earned $1.50–2.00 goes into the bank.

In many modern societies there is a tendency

among ordinary folk to believe that saving is an unmitigated good, and consumption something to be done furtively and out of sight. This tendency was reversed somewhat in the 1980s when bold "conspicuous consumers" came out of the closet. But the "negative nineties" have brought back the idea that diligent saving is the only redemption for the sin of consumption.

The Economist once said: "Saving is not a virtue in itself – a public good to be encouraged by government, like careful driving or using litter bins. It is an economic decision about the alloca- tion of resources." If everybody's decision were to save half their income, we would all be in a sorry state.

Prices and sources

Anything that is not consumed is, by definition, saved; and the decision whether to consume or to save is based largely on price. The price of savings in this case is the general level of real interest rates, that is, nominal rates less inflation. Histori- cally these have fluctuated between -4% (in the USA in the 1970s) and 8% (in the USA in the mid-1980s).

Anything too far outside this range is unsustain- able. A market with persistently negative real rates is soon going to run out of savers; and one with real rates in double figures is going to be hard-pressed to find profitable homes for the high level of savings that would be attracted to such rates.

Savings come essentially from individuals and from companies. They can, in theory, also come from governments, but it is a rare government these days that is not borrowing from others in order to pay its bills.

Although governments and government institu- tions are not themselves great savers, they do have great influence on the direction in which savings flow, for the following reasons:

- Their budget deficits make them large consumers of others' savings;
- National savings schemes' interest rates can

be insensitive to market forces. They can thus shift the competitive position of different private-sector financial institutions;

- By the structure of their tax systems, governments almost invariably encourage borrowing at the expense of savings. Not for them the guilt of excessive consumption and inadequate saving.

In a world of nation states, each state can also attract savings from foreigners. If governments permit (that is, if they remove exchange controls), nations can export or import savings just as easily as they can export or import consumer goods. If left alone, savings will flow across the exchanges from one nation to another in search of the highest rate of return.

The intermediaries

There is a host of institutions keen to be the bearer of these savings to those borrowers judged capable of using them productively. These institutions compete with each other, and dangle a different balance of risk and reward with which to entice savings their way.

They fall into a number of categories.

Short-term financial markets. These provide the savers and users of funds with a direct interface. They include markets as short-term as the overnight interbank market, in which banks place their surplus funds for the overnight use of other banks with a shortage. They also include markets for instruments like commercial paper (a means for companies to place their surpluses with other companies) and treasury bills (which enable governments to raise funds from individuals and financial institutions). Commercial paper and treasury bills can have a maturity of three months and more.

Bond markets and stockmarkets. These are long-term financial markets. Bonds can be issued with a maturity of anything up to 15 years, and shares are issued for eternity. Investors deterred by the thought of being locked into financial assets for so long are given reassurance by the existence of secondary markets. These provide liquidity at all times; that is, they enable investors to sell their long-term assets at short-term notice (though maybe at a loss) whenever they wish.

Banks and other short-term financial institutions. Basic commercial banks provide savers with a number of different services, from very short-term current accounts to longer-term time deposits. They also provide the core service of money transmission. This enables savers to move money from one institution to another without having to carry bundles of notes from door to door.

Traditionally, banks come in a number of different guises depending on whether their key function is money transmission (commercial banks); the collection of savings (savings banks); the raising of money in financial markets for industry and governments (investment banks); or all of these things (universal banks). In recent years these distinctions have become less and less clear.

Long-term financial institutions. These consist mainly of insurance companies and pension funds, institutions that have become the biggest repositories of developed nations' savings. They collect huge sums of money which they invest mostly in stock and bond markets. In many places tax advantages have greatly enhanced the attractiveness of these institutions as conduits for savings (see also essay on page 20).

THE LIMITS TO GLOBALISATION

There has been a remarkable shift in recent years in the progress of globalisation among financial-service firms. In the 1980s western banks seemed to recognise few boundaries, lending vast sums to countries as far apart as Argentina and South Korea, and opening branches in cities from Chicago to Singapore. In the 1990s, however, many of these banks have been busily retrenching. The number of overseas branches of American banks declined from over 900 in 1985 to under 750 a decade later. The number of staff working for foreign banks in London also fell sharply over the same period.

Globalisation has fallen well down the list of most financial institutions' strategic priorities. Japanese banks, once the most enthusiastic of globetrotters, have been grounded by a series of disastrous results. In the year to March 1996, for example, 16 out of the top 20 Japanese banks reported losses.

In Europe, a recent survey carried out by the Paris-based European Financial Management and Marketing Associate (EFMA) found that retail banks are focused on improving their domestic operations rather than on looking for new opportunities abroad. Almost three-quarters of them said that they did not expect their bank to have a significant retail presence outside its national boundaries by the year 2005.

"Many banks lured overseas during the 1980s have failed (to accelerate the bank's growth and to increase its ROE, its return on equity)," said the report. "Scaling down international assets and offices seems more the pattern for banks today."

By and large, the opportunities presented by the EU's so-called "single passport directive" – which permits an institution that is authorised to carry out banking business in one member state to do so in all member states – have not been taken. High-profile cross-border deals, like those between Deutsche Bank and Morgan Grenfell and between Dresdner Bank and Kleinwort Benson, have shown that it is easy to underestimate potential cross-cultural conflicts. And those conflicts may arise as much from commercial banks going into investment banking (or insurance) as from one national culture blending with another.

American banks too are drawing in their horns in order to concentrate on their domestic market. Interstate banking, for so long banned in the United States, was finally approved by Congress in 1995 and went into full effect from June 1997. Mega-mergers among US banks (between Chase and Chemical, for instance, and Wells Fargo – the world's most profitable bank in 1995 – and First Interstate, a name that speaks for itself) are indicative of the way that the industry there is gearing up for new domestic opportunities.

American banks are particularly concerned about the way in which their domestic credit-card business has slipped out of their grasp in recent years. Non-traditional firms like Dean Witter's Discover and First USA have more than doubled their market share between 1992 and 1997. Over the same period, the share of the leading commercial banks was halved. (With 39 million cardholders, Dean Witter's Discover was in 1997 the biggest credit-card operation in the world.)

The banks want to claw back their lost market share, and recently some of the non-traditional card businesses have been brought back into the banking fold: in early 1997, for example, Morgan Stanley merged with Dean Witter Discover, and Banc One of Columbus Ohio bought First USA (for $6.65 billion).

The insurance industry has remained more gung-ho about globalisation than the bankers. A few prominent companies (like the French group UAP and America's AIG) have spread themselves far and wide. But for the most part they have taken over local operations which have continued to trade in much the same way as they did when they were locally owned.

Stockmarkets

The area where globalisation has taken place in the financial field in the 1990s is the stockmarket. Nowadays stocks and shares are sold around the world as casually as bank loans used to be syndicated. It has been estimated that one out of every seven equity trades carried out today involves a foreigner. Ten years ago Salomon Brothers reckoned that 99% of the world's equity trading was done on the exchange where shares had their primary listing. That is a very significant shift.

The world's major stock exchanges have been at the forefront of the internationalisation. The New York Stock Exchange (NYSE), the world's premier exchange with its access to the unmatchable pool of US capital, has led the trend, first through its use of the American Depositary Receipt (ADR), and then through the growing number of foreign companies prepared to go to the not inconsiderable expense of obtaining a full listing on the NYSE.

The London Stock Exchange – which briefly (until it was disallowed) changed its name to the International Stock Exchange – is still the world's most international market. Almost 40% of its turnover now comes from non-UK clients buying non-UK equity, and another quarter comes from UK clients buying non-UK equity.

Then again, much of the growth that has occurred in recent years in the emerging stockmarkets of the developing world has come from overseas. Special funds set up in Europe and America to give risk-loving investors in those countries access to more exotic markets like Mumbai and Istanbul have proved very popular. It does not take much American investment to move market indices in these places sharply, and more than half of all US pension funds now have some assets invested in emerging markets' securities.

There are those who maintain that the Internet will give financial institutions of all shapes and sizes fantastic opportunities to play on a truly international stage. Consulting firm Ernst & Young, for example, has said that "on-line real-time banking across all time zones now appears to be only a question of resources and political barriers – not insignificant obstacles, but ones that are likely to be overcome in the near future".

Hundreds of banks, most of them American, already have "sites" on the Internet's World Wide Web, and many of them are exploring the possibility of carrying out transactions on the Internet. In Ernst & Young's assessment "non-bank entities are positioning themselves to use the same infrastructure to provide similar quasi-bank capabilities".

Security problems have yet to be overcome before the Internet can become a widely popular channel for delivering financial services. But when they are overcome, there will be few limits on where that channel can reach. It may not be long before a housewife in Warsaw can get her car insurance from a supermarket in San Francisco – via the Internet.

THE CONVERGENCE OF CORPORATE FINANCE

A nation depends critically upon its ability to provide its manufacturing and service industries with the finance that they need in order to generate greater profits and greater wealth. Nevertheless, despite this common purpose, nations have developed very different ways in which to channel funds to their industries.

In some cases these ways have evolved over more than a century. But in recent years they have been changing rapidly, and in one direction. Corporate finance all over the globe has been converging onto a single model – that of the United States.

Historically the most fundamental difference in corporate finance was found in the relative roles of banks and of stockmarkets. In industrially successful nations like Germany and Japan, industry's relationship with banks was very close. For example, a quarter of Germany's biggest industrial company, Daimler-Benz, has for years been owned by Deutsche Bank, the country's biggest commercial bank. Not only has Daimler-Benz relied almost exclusively on Deutsche for all its banking needs, but the chairman of Deutsche Bank has been, almost *ex officio*, the chairman of the supervisory board of Daimler-Benz.

In Japan, most big companies have one so-called main bank. As in Germany, the main bank and the company may well be linked by an equity stake, and the company will invariably rely on its main bank for all its short-term financing needs.

In Anglo-Saxon economies, however, the picture is rather different. There, industry relies much more on financial markets for money than financial institutions. Corporate bonds and shares account for a far higher percentage of Anglo-Saxon companies' external sources of funds.

Relatively heavy dependence on financial markets brings demands that can be quite as exacting as those of a German or a Japanese bank. Top of the list is the remorseless payment of dividends, which public companies feel unable to forgo for fear that their value in the market (their market capitalisation) will be cut. A lower capitalisation means a higher cost of raising new equity.

So you have the situation where steady annual dividends are being paid to supposedly risk-taking Anglo-Saxon investors out of money that could otherwise have become (cheap) internal funds for financing investment. On occasions, companies have been known to go as far as to borrow from their banks in order to maintain the level of their dividends.

Greater dependence on financial markets does, however, free Anglo-Saxon industry from its bankers. Big US companies shop around for banking services and may use literally hundreds of banks, each for a different bit of business. Add to that the fact that staff turnover at US banks is much faster than it is in Germany or Japan, and the finance executives of US corporations can find themselves dealing with several different account officers at a bank in as many months. In Germany and Japan bank employees still look upon their jobs as life-time employment. They expect to be serving the same customers for decades.

Following the Anglo-Saxons

All this is changing very rapidly, though, with the perceived success of American-style capitalism in general, and of the Anglo-Saxon model of corporate finance in particular. There is little need to look further than Daimler-Benz to see the extent of the change.

Over the past few years Germany's largest industrial company has listed its shares on the New York Stock Exchange (with all the disclosure requirements which that entails); it has adopted American-style accounting standards; and (perhaps most revolutionary of all) it has linked its senior managers' pay to changes in the company's share price. Meanwhile its bank, Deutsche Bank, has bought the British investment bank Morgan Grenfell, an institution which lives off its ability to sell corporate securities, not loans.

This conversion to Anglo-Saxon finance has been brought about by a number of wider changes that have been taking place in the business world.

In the first instance, the deregulation of financial markets has, among other things, removed restrictions on the amount of interest that banks can pay to depositors. It has also introduced greater competition into the markets for deposits and loans. This has inevitably pushed up the price of loans and encouraged companies to seek funds from outside the banking system.

Partly as a consequence of deregulation, industrial companies have found that they are increasingly able to cut banks out of the chain that passes money from an original lender to an ultimate borrower. This process is known as disintermediation, and was first strikingly demonstrated by the growth of the commercial paper market in the United States. Commercial paper is a short-term financial instrument issued by corporations, and among the biggest buyers of commercial paper are other (non-financial) corporations.

Disintermediation has now spread beyond the United States. Companies in Europe (including Daimler-Benz) can often borrow more cheaply in short-term financial markets than they can from banks. This can be seen as part of a wider trend among all businesses – the trend to squeeze out middle-men wherever possible in the drive to cut costs. So-called "financial intermediaries" are, by definition, middle-men.

The extraordinary popularity of privatisation across the world has been another influence changing the face of corporate finance. Privatisation has not only sharply increased the amount of equity traded on stockmarkets, from London to Taipei, but it has also increased corporations' awareness of the benefits of equity financing as against debt.

Finally, further promoting this message (and the American capitalist philosophy in general) has been the army of investment bankers and management consultants that have been spreading across the globe in search of business for more than a decade.

The investment bankers came first. Firms like Salomon Brothers and Morgan Stanley crossed the Atlantic in the early 1980s and used London as a springboard for selling securities-based services to corporations throughout continental Europe and beyond.

They were followed by the management consultants, firms like McKinsey and the Boston Consulting Group. Their mission was to sell grand financial strategies based on models that had been drawn up by academics at American business schools, and at Harvard in particular. Those models were firmly rooted in American business experience only.

The diaspora of these consultants led one European to comment that American-style capitalism was not being spread by word of mouth; it was being sold.

The missionaries for American capitalism have been able to export their strategies around the world because so much of the rest of the world has come to believe that America has got it right in promoting the interests of the shareholder above those of others with a stake in the corporation. The more that those other stakeholders (employees, banks, etc) can be converted into shareholders, the more popular the idea will become.

PENSION FUNDS

One group of financial institutions that is sure to come more into the limelight in the early years of the 21st century is the pension funds. These sleeping giants are already enormous – the total assets of the top 1,000 US pension funds alone were put at $3.4 trillion at the end of 1996. And every year the funds record real rates of growth that stretch into double figures.

As long ago as 1979, Harold Wilson, a British prime minister, was saying that "the growth of pension funds during the 1970s has created the biggest revolution in the British financial scene this century. Surprisingly, it was almost totally unperceived by political or even financial commentators until very recently."

Since then, pension funds have grown exponentially, and not just in the developed world. In the early 1980s Chile showed the way for a number of developing countries to establish widespread private pension schemes.

While the funds invest in a variety of assets (British Rail's pension fund once had a widely publicised binge into paintings and sculpture) the great majority of the savings that pours into them gets invested in the major bond and stockmarkets of the western world. Even in Chile, where private pension funds were prohibited from investing abroad until 1991, the funds are largely invested in stocks or bonds, be they domestic or foreign.

Some argue that this has encouraged the development of domestic "emerging" capital markets, although a recent study by the OECD cast doubt on this by finding a negative correlation between the size of a country's pension-fund assets and the growth of its stockmarket's capitalisation and turnover.

The funds come under fire
The stellar performance of pension funds throughout the world has, however, been accompanied by a growing unease among the general

public about these institutions. A series of scandals (ranging from the misleading selling of pensions to the ease with which light-fingered individuals have been able to get their hands on pension fund money) has left a large question mark over the regulation of the funds.

Moreover, publicity about the seven-figure salaries that the managers of allegedly successful funds can earn has made people wonder whether the tax benefits (that are usually the main selling point of pensions) are not being eaten up in unseemly management fees. Might savers not be better off leaving their money in a bank or in a second home?

Finally, the funds have been seen to have stood feebly on the sidelines when major issues of corporate governance have been raised by company behaviour. They are the biggest members of a privileged group (ie, shareholders). Why are they so unwilling to shoulder the responsibility that comes with that privilege?

Confronting the issues

First, the issue of regulation. It is not, it would seem, a case of there not being enough regulation. In the UK, for example, it is reckoned that compliance costs amount to some 9% of the industry's turnover, a high figure by any standards.

It is more a case of it being the wrong sort of regulation. What the industry needs, it is argued, is not more confidential forms to be sent to regulators but more openness and more competition.

The industry is notoriously secretive. It is, for example, often difficult to get an actuarial valuation from a manager of a fund to which the inquirer may have been contributing for many years and which may, at the end of the day, be his or her main source of retirement income. And the structure of fees charged for fund management is often less than straightforward for non-experts to understand.

The secrecy of the industry has helped to reduce competition. But an increasing number of non-traditional suppliers of fund management services have at last been attracted by the profits to be made in the business, and they are now looking to get a slice of it. These suppliers include high-street banks, "direct" sales operations, and maverick organisations like Richard Branson's Virgin. This is going to put pressure on the fund managers' margins and on the money available for their bonuses.

In their 1996 review of the investment management business in the UK, accountants Price Waterhouse found that costs in the industry had been rising much faster than inflation for the previous four years. It has been estimated that up to 20% of the annual contributions to UK personal pension plans can go in marketing and management costs, compared with about 1–2% for state pensions.

The major element of costs is salaries, and that includes the discretionary bonuses that are now the norm in the industry and which allow star managers to earn millions of dollars a year.

Price Waterhouse foresees a major problem "when discretionary bonuses become a normal and expected part of an individual's remuneration". Since bonuses are generally based on overall market performance rather than on the merit of any individual manager's research, timing, or efficiency, what is going to happen when the stockmarket falls? Are the tables going to be turned, with fund managers paying back to pensioners the management fees that have been the source of their extravagant bonuses in the past? It seems unlikely.

And then, finally, there is the vexed question of corporate governance. Pension funds are entrusted to act on behalf of the beneficiaries of the funds, and so they are subject to legal fiduciary requirements of prudence and care. In the past this has too often been an excuse for inaction.

In recent years, however, a small number of funds have made strategic decisions to become more involved in issues of corporate governance. This has been most evident in the United States, and particularly among union-sponsored and public-sector employees' funds. It has been partly sparked off by widespread concern at the extent of corporate "downsizing", and by rule changes making it easier for pension funds to make their case to other shareholders.

In the next century, pension fund managers will find it increasingly difficult to turn their backs on major issues affecting the corporations whose shares they hold. They are sure to become more active, more open, and less well-paid.

THE IMPACT OF INFORMATION TECHNOLOGY ON FINANCIAL SERVICES

Information technology (IT) has been the biggest single influence on the financial services industry in recent years. The convergence of computers and telecommunications that is the essence of IT has had some astonishing effects on the way in which financial services are delivered and on the way in which financial transactions are carried out. Consider the following:

- It is forecast that within a few years half of all car insurance in the UK will be sold over the telephone. Staff are already able to key a potential customer's details into a computer and receive a quotation in seconds. This kind of direct selling is hitting traditional insurance agents hard.
- The growing use of automated teller machines (ATMS) and other forms of electronic banking has led consultants Deloitte & Touche to predict that "modern high-street retail banks may be forced to sweep away up to 50% of their branch networks" if they are to survive the revolution in the industry that is being created by IT.
- On the world's major stock exchanges, trading in stocks and shares is no longer carried out on a traditional "floor". Brokers do not need to have eye contact any more in order to deal in securities. They can check the latest prices on a computer screen and do their deals over the telephone.

That financial services should have been affected more profoundly by IT than other industries should not be surprising. IT is about information, and the way in which the technology of the silicon chip can organise information and disseminate it at speeds undreamed of even only a few years ago when the IT revolution was already well established. The financial services industry is also first and foremost in the business of reorganising information – information about securities, cash or premiums – and of disseminating it quickly among buyers and sellers.

The sums being spent on IT are enormous and look set to grow even bigger. American commercial banks alone are reckoned to be spending in the region of $20 billion a year on IT. One estimate anticipates that total worldwide spending on IT by the finance industry in 1998 will be $300 billion. Europe is expected to account for 30% of that; the Americas for 45%; and Asia for 25%.

Undoubtedly much of this expenditure will be a waste of money. Gullible finance industry executives are being persuaded to part with large sums of money for complex IT systems which are far more sophisticated than they need, and which, in any case, they themselves are incapable of using and understanding. This is particularly true of banks and insurance companies in less developed markets.

Financial institutions are being persuaded to spend this money because they realise that IT is now central to their future strategy and to their survival. The dematerialisation of financial transactions (transferring into electronic form what used to be recorded on paper) has given a whole new range of competitors access to the financial services industry. For example, bank facilities of one sort or another are increasingly to be found inside supermarkets.

Most supermarkets have entered the business initially in partnership with traditional financial institutions because regulatory requirements still do not allow them to go it alone. But few doubt that the day will soon come when supermarkets can be banks in their own right.

One response to this threat is for banks to become supermarkets. In California Wells Fargo bank has begun to sell toothpaste and pharmaceutical products in a number of its branches.

Telecoms companies could be another group well placed to offer financial services. Inevitably, they would deliver the services "directly" – ie, over the telephone. And everybody in the industry believes it is only a matter of time before Bill Gates's Microsoft (and other software firms) target financial services as a promising new business area for them to enter.

For these new entrants there is no need to open expensive branches or set up a network of commission agents. They can operate from inexpensive call centres based in areas of high unemployment. From there, ranks of telephone operators can handle customer enquiries and requests from all over the world. Call centres do not need to be where the money is.

Existing financial institutions are already finding themselves faced with the considerable challenge of deciding what to do with the legacy of branches, staff and expensive property that their business has traditionally required. Many are closing branches and offices, and laying off staff on an unprecedented scale.

In an attempt to spend more wisely on IT (and to compensate for their own ignorance) many financial service firms have outsourced the management and development of their IT resources to others, firms like the American IT services giants EDS and Andersen Consulting. Mature financial businesses like cheque and credit-card processing, and the management of automated teller machines (ATMs), are these days largely in the hands of these specialist outsourcers. Even an institution as independent and conservative as the Swiss Bank Corporation has signed away the management of its computer systems for the next 25 years – to a company from Dallas called Perot Systems.

The sale of financial services over the Internet via home-based PCs is expected to provide the next dramatic change in the way that financial services are delivered to customers. At the moment, even in America less than 10% of households are wired up to the Internet, and there is still considerable concern about the confidentiality of financial information that has been fed into public networks (like the Internet).

But the exceptional cost savings that can be made from this form of delivery will be pushing the Internet's case strongly over the next few years. A study by consultants Booz-Allen & Hamilton reckons that banking transactions in America via the Internet will cost an average of $0.01. This compares with $0.54 for "direct" banking over the telephone, and $1.07 for a transaction carried out in the traditional way at a full-service bank branch. The virtual bank, electronic and incorporeal, is virtually upon us.

Part 2

A–Z

ACCEPTANCE

A BILL OF EXCHANGE that has been endorsed by a BANK; that is, a bank has given its GUARANTEE that it will pay the bill should the buyer fail to do so. This is a time-honoured way of financing trade. The exporter whose bill is accepted by a first-class bank can then sell the bill at a DISCOUNT in the financial markets. This improves the exporter's CASH FLOW over what it would have been had it waited for its customer to pay in the normal course of business.

ACCOUNT

The balance of a customer's borrowing and lending with a BANK. This type of account can take several forms.

- **Current account.** An account on which cheques can be drawn and an OVERDRAFT arranged. Current accounts do not usually pay significant amounts of INTEREST on positive balances. Charges (although rarely itemised) are usually related to the volume of transactions, the size of the balance on the account and the type of service provided.
- **Deposit account.** An account that is always kept in credit, and on which interest is paid.
- **Savings account.** An account designed specifically to assist customers to accumulate large sums by means of small and regular savings.
- **Budget account.** An account designed to help individuals make bulky bothersome payments (like telephone or electricity bills) more smoothly. Regular payments into the account allow the account-holder to borrow several times the value of each payment. Sometimes such an account is in credit; sometimes it is overdrawn. The plan, however, is that it should have the same balance at the end of a year as it has at the beginning.

ACCRUAL RATE

The rate at which a pension increases each year, usually expressed as a fraction. Most people are part of a one-eightieth or one-sixtieth pension scheme. This means that for each year that they are in the scheme they receive one-eightieth or one-sixtieth of their pensionable earnings on retirement.

ACCRUED INTEREST

The interest that has been earned, but not yet paid, on a bond or loan. Bonds may pay interest only half-yearly or quarterly. However, 170 days after the most recent half-yearly interest payment has been made, a considerable amount of (unpaid) interest has accrued.

ACTUAL

The physical COMMODITY or SECURITY underlying a FUTURES contract.

ACTUARIAL SURPLUS

See OVERFUNDING.

ACTUARY

Facetiously described as someone who finds accounting too exciting. Actuaries contemplate (then calculate) the probability of death occurring to others within prescribed periods of time. This enables INSURANCE companies and the like to determine what PREMIUM they should charge to those taking out life-assurance policies.

ADJUSTABLE RATE MORTGAGE

A type of MORTGAGE whose RATE OF INTEREST varies over time, and in line with market rates. Historically, mortgages in the USA have been predominantly fixed-rate. On occasions of great interest-rate turbulence this type of mortgage has got financial institutions into trouble when they have been unable to find suitable liabilities to match their fixed-rate assets.

Institutions which do grant adjustable rate mortgages (ARMS) like to issue long-term bonds to match the rate and MATURITY of the loans they are granting. In the UK the great majority of mortgages are ARMS.

ADR
See AMERICAN DEPOSITARY RECEIPT.

ADVANCE/DECLINE RATIO
A measure of the difference between the number of stocks whose price is rising on a market, and the number whose price is falling. In the USA when this difference itself starts to fall it is believed to indicate that a market has peaked.

AFLOATS
Commodities that are on board a ship, shipshape and ready to sail.

AFTER-HOURS
Shares that are bought and sold after an official STOCK EXCHANGE has officially closed (usually about 15.30). After-hours trades are treated as having been executed on the following day.

AGENT
Someone who acts on behalf of others. For example, an estate agent attempting to sell a property on behalf of the owner, for a fee or for a percentage of the sale price.

The word has a special meaning on the LLOYD'S insurance market. It is someone who introduces a member (or NAME) to the market, and advises him or her about it.

AIBD
See ASSOCIATION OF INTERNATIONAL BOND DEALERS.

AIM
The Alternative Investment Market, the junior arm of the London Stock Exchange, designed to be a cheaper and easier source of new capital for small, young companies than the main London stockmarket.

AIM replaced the Unlisted Securities Market

(USM), which had been set up in 1980 with much the same aim as AIM. However, the USM became increasingly indistinguishable from the main London market, and demand to be listed on it fell sharply.

ALLFINANZ
An Anglo-German neologism for the coming together of banking and INSURANCE services under one institutional umbrella. Many such institutions have been formed by merger; others by a joint venture between a BANK and an insurance company. Some (like Germany's Deutsche Bank) preferred to go into the new service (in its case insurance) from scratch.

The benefit of Allfinanz is said to come from selling in the same outlet such compatible retail products as consumer loans and life assurance. Yet the two have traditionally been sold in very different ways: the consumer LOAN in a bank BRANCH; life assurance in the customer's own home. Although insurance is increasingly being sold in bank branches, and consumer CREDIT in other ways (for example, by direct mail), changing customers' minds about how they should buy financial products is a slow process.

ALLOTMENT
The amount of STOCK that is allocated to subscribers when an ISSUE of securities is OVERSUBSCRIBED.

It is also the amount of stock that is given to each member of a SYNDICATE when a new issue is syndicated.

ALPHA STOCK
The most actively traded shares on the London STOCKMARKET. A category devised by SEAQ, it consists of shares in which a continuous TWO-WAY MARKET is guaranteed by market makers. The specific shares that are included in the Alpha group can change from time to time.

ALTERNATIVE INVESTMENT
A less immediately obvious way of retaining value

than securities and BANK deposits; for example, works of art, coins, stamps, jewels or GOLD. Alternative investments tend to outperform more traditional investments when INFLATION rates are high.

AMERICAN DEPOSITARY RECEIPT

A certificate issued in the USA in lieu of a foreign SECURITY. The original securities are lodged in a BANK abroad, and the American depositary receipts (ADRS) are traded in the USA to all intents and purposes as if they were a domestic STOCK.

An ADR'S DIVIDEND is paid in US dollars, so it provides a way for (parochial) American investors to buy foreign securities without having to go abroad, and without having to switch into foreign currencies.

An increasing number of foreign companies are quoted on US exchanges in their own right. But that is an expensive process, and only an option for those who can cope with the seemingly insatiable demand for information of the SECURITIES AND EXCHANGE COMMISSION and other US regulatory bodies.

The traditional market leader in issuing ADRS is Morgan Guaranty Bank, which effectively invented them in 1927. There are now over 120 ADRS quoted on the NEW YORK STOCK EXCHANGE, AMEX and NASDAQ; one-third of them are British.

The American Express salad oil incident is one of financial history's most notorious scams. A client borrowed substantial sums of money against the security of huge tanks of salad oil. When the client disappeared, the tanks turned out to be filled with water. A drop or two of oil had been left floating on the top of each one – all that could be seen by the casual observer.

AMERICAN STOCK EXCHANGE

The USA's second-biggest STOCK EXCHANGE (after the NEW YORK STOCK EXCHANGE). Also based in New York, the American Stock Exchange concentrates on the shares of medium-sized companies that are too small to justify the full expense of a LISTING on the NYSE.

The American Stock Exchange is commonly known as AMEX and less commonly as the Kerb Exchange, a name that was officially dropped in 1953.

AMEX
See previous entry.

ANALYST
A person who studies the progress of companies and of industries in order to make judgments and recommendations about the value of different stocks and shares, or about the creditworthiness of different DEBT instruments. Such analysts normally work for financial firms like stockbrokers and INSURANCE companies.

The word analyst is also used to refer to those people who analyse markets from inside manufacturing companies.

The largest attendance at an annual general meeting occurred in April 1961 when 20,100 shareholders turned up for the AGM of AT&T, the American Telephone and Telegraph Company.

ANNUALISED PERCENTAGE RATE
A standardised measure of the annual RATE OF INTEREST which enables rates on different instruments to be compared. Before the annualised percentage rate (APR) became established as the yardstick for such comparisons, there were many alternative ways of expressing interest rates. Consumers could be easily confused by LOAN sharks comparing interest-rate "apples" with interest-rate "pears".

The APR is calculated by the formula:

$$\text{APR} = \left[(1 + \tfrac{x}{100})^y - 1 \right]$$

where x is the rate of interest quoted for a period of less than a year (for example, 2% a month); and y is the number of such periods in a year.

ANNUITY

Originally an investment that bought a fixed annual payment for the investor (called the annuitant) until his or her death. A number of complications have been added on to that basic format. For example, the payment of the benefit is nowadays more likely to be quarterly or semi-annual than annual.

There is also a wide range of specialised annuities.

- **Joint annuity.** The benefit is paid throughout the lifetime of two people (usually husband and wife) and continues until both are dead.
- **Tontine annuity.** A joint annuity where the payment increases as the number of annuitants decreases (that is, when the husband dies the wife gets a bigger regular payment).
- **Deferred annuity.** The regular payments do not begin until after a certain specified period.
- **Perpetual annuity.** The payments go on for ever (to survivors that is).

APPLICATION FORM

Part of the PROSPECTUS for a new ISSUE; that part of it which has to be filled in and returned by those who wish to buy some of the issue. For large new issues, application forms are sometimes published as advertisements in newspapers.

APR

See ANNUALISED PERCENTAGE RATE.

ARBITRAGE

The buying and selling of financial instruments on different markets in order to take advantage of price differences between the markets. The markets may be in different countries (the FOREIGN-EXCHANGE markets in London and New York, for instance); or they may just be different markets in the same country.

A typical arbitrage deal might involve buying all the shares of a company quoted on the NEW YORK STOCK EXCHANGE, and reorganising it into three separate bits: one to be sold to a Swiss investor, one to a UK quoted company and one to be floated separately on the AMERICAN STOCK EXCHANGE.

A person who lives by arbitrage is called an arbitrageur.

ARM
See ADJUSTABLE RATE MORTGAGE.

ASSET-BACKED SECURITY
A SECURITY that is issued by a financial institution and backed by assets (such as a number of mortgages or of car loans) that are on the institution's balance sheet. The assets are placed in trust, and the investor in the security can look to them (and sometimes only to them) for repayment of its INTEREST and PRINCIPAL.

ASSET COVER
The number of times that a company's DEBT is covered by its NET assets.

ASSET MANAGEMENT
The art of getting the best return possible from the (financial) assets that an institution owns or manages. This involves finding the ideal balance between the yield from the assets on the one hand, and their RISK, MATURITY and LIQUIDITY on the other.

Financial institutions used to devote much attention to asset management. When there was little competition for savers' deposits, their liabilities took care of themselves. But with the rapid DEREGULATION of financial markets in the 1980s, competition for deposits and savings grew rapidly. With it grew the amount of attention paid to the different game of LIABILITY MANAGEMENT.

ASSET STRIPPER
A person who buys a company in order to make a PROFIT by peeling off its assets bit by bit, and

then selling them. These assets may be separate subsidiaries, or plant and equipment, or property. This process invariably involves the stripping of another sort of asset (the employees) of a number of jobs. This has been largely responsible for giving asset strippers a bad name.

The asset stripper relies on there being a difference in the price of the business as a whole (as valued by a STOCKMARKET, for example) and the sum of the amounts that can be raised for its parts sold separately. Such a possibility arises most commonly when a company is making losses, or a much smaller profit than seems to be justified by its size.

ASSET VALUE
The market value of all the securities and CASH held by an INVESTMENT TRUST on a particular day, usually expressed as so much per SHARE.

ASSOCIATION OF INTERNATIONAL BOND DEALERS
See INTERNATIONAL SECURITIES MARKET ASSOCIATION.

AT BEST
An order from a customer to a BROKER to buy or sell a certain SECURITY at the best current price available.

ATM
See following entry.

AUTOMATED TELLER MACHINE
A machine that can carry out most of the functions of a BANK teller or cashier. Automated teller machines (ATMs) should be distinguished from CASH dispensers: dispensers only dispense cash; ATMs do much more. They take orders for cheque books, hand out statements and even take in deposits.

Over the past two decades ATMs have been spreading like ivy, through banks' walls and inside their branches.

AVAL
A sort of continental European ACCEPTANCE; a GUAR-

ANTEE stamped on a BILL OF EXCHANGE. It guarantees that a trusted party (such as a BANK) will meet the liability if called upon. The bank usually signs or stamps its name under the words *Pour Aval* or *Bon Pour Aval*.

AVERAGE COST

See MARGINAL COST.

AVERAGING

The process of buying more of a certain type of SECURITY as its price falls in order to reduce the average price paid for the security. For example, suppose a speculator pays $5 a SHARE for 10,000 shares in First National Bank of Nowhere just before the BANK is linked with massive and criminal laundering of drug money. The bank's share price plunges to $1. The speculator might then decide to buy 10,000 more shares at $1 each.

The speculator has thus paid $60,000 for 20,000 shares, averaging the cost per share at $3 and enabling them to be sold at a PROFIT as soon as the price of NatBank of Nowhere rises above $3.

BACK-TO-BACK

COLLATERAL provided by importers to back CREDIT extended to them by exporters. In the case of importers in developing countries who are buying from developed countries where they are not known, such collateral could be something like a bank DEPOSIT held abroad by the importer.

BACKWARDATION

The situation where a COMMODITY due for delivery today fetches a higher price than the same commodity to be delivered at a future date. Backwardation usually occurs where there are temporary log-jams in transport or distribution, which make the commodity temporarily rare.

BAD DEBT

A LOAN or a bill that is not paid within a reasonable time of its due-by date, usually because a borrower has gone bankrupt or a customer has CASH-FLOW problems. Bad debts are an inevitable part of business; keeping them under control is an art.

Banks set aside PROVISIONS out of their regular PROFIT to cover the bad debts that they know they will suffer. Without provisions, all of a bad debt has to be taken out of profit in the year in which it occurs.

BALANCE SHEET

That part of a company's accounts which lists its assets and its liabilities. Fundamental to all such accounts is the idea that assets and liabilities are equal – ie, that they are in balance. However, this is a truism, since the difference between them is called "shareholders' funds", and this amounts to whatever is needed to put them in balance.

BALLOON

A LOAN whose repayments are not spread evenly over its life. At one stage – towards the loan's MATURITY – the regular dribble of repayments bulges into one or two big balloon repayments that finally wipe the slate clean.

BANK

An institution that deals in money and (most significantly) creates money by making loans that do not have to be repaid until some future date. Because of this function, governments have always kept a close eye on their banks.

There are many types of bank (see CENTRAL BANK, CLEARING BANK, CONSORTIUM BANK, INVESTMENT BANK, MERCHANT BANK, MONEY-CENTER BANK, MUTUAL SAVINGS BANK, PRIVATE BANK, SAVINGS BANK, UNIVERSAL BANK) and the main difference between them is the amount of emphasis that they place on various fundamental banking services. These include the following.

1 Collecting deposits from savers and paying INTEREST on those deposits (the cost of having the use of the money over time).

2 Granting loans to borrowers who seem likely to make good use of them. This is what banks do in order to earn enough interest to pay their depositors.

3 Money transmission. A service which enables customers of one bank to transfer funds directly from their account to the account of somebody else at another bank. This service is provided by means of things like a CHEQUE, STANDING ORDER and DIRECT DEBIT.

4 Advisory services. In particular, advising companies on how and where to raise new CAPITAL, and then arranging for the capital to be raised.

5 Lending their good name to help customers that they trust. This is fundamental to trade finance. An exporter gives CREDIT to an importer because the importer's bank gives its word to the exporter's bank that payment will be forthcoming. The two banks trust each other; if the importer and exporter did too they would not need the banks.

6 Providing services to other banks in order, for example, for them to clear funds among themselves. This is a principal function of central banks.

The first three of these services are fundamental to

the business of commercial banks; the fourth and fifth are fee-earning services that are at the heart of the business of merchant banks.

Nowadays banks offer a lot more besides. In California, Wells Fargo bank even sells toothpaste.

Banks are dinosaurs. Give me a piece of the transaction business, and they're history.
Bill Gates, chairman and co-founder of Microsoft

BANK FOR INTERNATIONAL SETTLEMENTS

A CENTRAL BANK for central bankers, based in Switzerland. It is a meeting place, a multinational regulatory authority and a CLEARING HOUSE for many nations' RESERVES.

Housed in a round tower near Basel railway station, the Bank for International Settlements (BIS) was set up in 1930 as a private company owned by a number of central banks, one commercial bank (Citibank) and some private individuals.

In the international DEBT crisis of the early 1980s the BIS played a vital role in supplying SHORT-TERM bridging loans that gave dollar-less developing countries time to adjust their economic policies. In the late 1980s it played a less conspicuous role in setting up an international safety net for rapidly deregulating financial markets.

BANK INSURANCE FUND

See FEDERAL DEPOSIT INSURANCE CORPORATION.

BANKER'S ACCEPTANCE

See ACCEPTANCE.

BANKER'S DRAFT

An order from a buyer or importer to its BANK instructing it to make a payment to the seller or exporter's bank. The draft is sent to the seller, which presents it to its bank for payment. The seller's bank in turn presents it to the buyer's bank for reimbursement.

BANKRUPTCY

The condition of a bankrupt, that is, a person who has been adjudged to be unable to pay his or her debts by a court. A bankrupt is deprived of many powers; for example, he or she cannot be a director of a company for a number of years. A bankrupt's property passes into the hands of a TRUSTEE in bankruptcy who is authorised to divide it among the creditors.

In the last four days of September 1857 150 banks failed in Rhode Island, Maryland, Virginia and Pennsylvania alone.

BARGAIN

A deal done at a good price. Also any transaction in stocks and shares on the INTERNATIONAL STOCK EXCHANGE in London.

BARTER

Paying for goods with other goods or services. Barter is at least as old as the Asian silk routes, and often just as devious. It enjoyed a renaissance with the opening up of the former Soviet Union and eastern Europe, regions with a huge demand for imports (particularly of capital goods) but with little foreign currency to pay for them.

Financial institutions are not too keen on barter since it threatens greatly to reduce the need for their services. Some financial institutions, however, have decided that if you cannot beat 'em, join 'em. They have set up specialist barter departments to organise and service the complicated deals that are increasingly being put together.

The biggest recorded barter deal was of 36m barrels of oil for ten Boeing 747 jets for Royal Saudi Airline in the 1980s.

BASIS POINT

A unit of measure used to express small movements in the rate of interest, foreign-exchange rates, or bond yields. One basis point is one-hundredth of one percentage point. Thus the differential between a bond yield of 5.38% and one of 5.79% is 41 basis points.

BASIS PRICE

See STRIKE PRICE.

BEAR

An investor who thinks that the price of an individual SECURITY (or of a whole market) is going to fall. A bear, therefore, sells securities in anticipation of being able to rebuy them later at a lower price.

Alternatively, bears will buy FUTURES contracts that commit them to selling securities at a fixed price on a future date. They anticipate that this fixed price will be higher than what they will have to pay for the securities in the spot market on that future date.

A bear market is one that is experiencing a sustained fall in prices. (See also BULL.)

BEARER SECURITY

A BOND or SHARE certificate that is not registered in the name of its owner. Whoever holds the certificate (or bears it) can collect the INTEREST or DIVIDEND due, usually by detaching a COUPON. A bearer security can be bought or sold without being endorsed; it is as liquid as CASH, and equally vulnerable to theft.

A EUROBOND is a bearer bond. Bearer bonds have the great advantage of being more easily kept out of the tax authorities' eye than normal registered securities.

BED AND BREAKFASTING

An expression referring to the practice of selling securities on the last day of a tax year and buying them back the next day (the first day of the next tax year). This is done to establish a loss for the first tax year which can then be set off against gains for the purposes of capital gains tax.

BELLWETHER

A SECURITY that is seen as a significant indicator of the direction in which a market's prices are moving. For example, AT&T'S SHARE price is a bellwether for the NEW YORK STOCK EXCHANGE; ICI'S share price likewise for the LONDON STOCK EXCHANGE. Long-term government bonds of various maturities are usually the bellwethers for national BOND markets.

BELLS AND WHISTLES

The little extras that are added to basic financial products. For example, the warrants or options that can be attached to simple bonds.

BENEFICIAL OWNER

The ultimate owner of a SECURITY, that is, the person who is entitled to receive the benefits associated with the security. The expression is applied in cases where a security is registered in the name of a custodian, someone who holds it in trust for the beneficial owner.

BERNE UNION

An association of providers of EXPORT CREDIT insurance. Founded in 1934, it aims to promote "the international acceptance of sound principles of export credit and INSURANCE".

BETA

A category of shares created by SEAQ. Beta stock is less actively traded than ALPHA STOCK.

BETA COEFFICIENT

See VOLATILITY.

BID

The highest price that a prospective buyer is prepared at that moment to pay for something, be it a company, a Van Gogh painting, or a SECURITY.

BID COSTS

The costs incurred by a company in bidding for another company. These include the fees of a panoply of advisers such as merchant bankers, lawyers and accountants. Bid costs have to be borne whether a bid is successful or not.

BID-OFFER SPREAD

The difference between the lowest price at which a seller will offer goods or services, and the highest price that a buyer will bid for them. In the FOR-EIGN-EXCHANGE market, for example, banks' exchange-rate quotations give two prices: the highest price that the BANK (as a buyer) will offer for a particular currency; and the lowest price it will accept for that currency (as a seller).

BIG BANG

What occurs on the day when a significant financial market removes a swathe of old-fashioned rules and regulations. The most famous Big Bang occurred at the London Stock Exchange on October 27th 1986. From that date:

- stockbrokers were obliged to abandon their long-standing fixed scale of COMMISSION;
- for the first time foreigners were allowed to own a majority stake in a UK BROKER; and
- DUAL CAPACITY was introduced, allowing brokers to be market makers and vice-versa.

The biggest bang on the day, however, came from the STOCK EXCHANGE's newly computerised dealing and quotations system which collapsed under the strain.

The US equivalent was called Mayday and took place on May 1st 1975, the day on which minimum commissions were abolished on the NEW YORK STOCK EXCHANGE.

BILL OF EXCHANGE

A written instruction to a buyer (importer) to pay a seller (exporter) a defined amount of money before a certain date. In the UK a CHEQUE is a bill of exchange, still governed in important respects by the Bills of Exchange Act of 1882.

BILL OF LADING
The set of documents giving title to goods while they are in transit. On the documents is a brief description of the goods and where they are going. The bill of lading is signed by the shipper, which undertakes to deliver the goods in the same condition as it receives them.

BIS
See BANK FOR INTERNATIONAL SETTLEMENTS.

BLACK MONDAY
STOCKMARKET history is riddled with black days. Black Monday was October 19th 1987, when virtually all the world's stockmarkets tumbled by all-time record amounts.

Black Tuesday was October 29th 1929, the blackest day of the Great Crash; others talk of Black Thursday, October 24th 1929, the day when the markets first began to fall heavily.

The UK has a Black Wednesday, September 9th 1992, the day when FOREIGN-EXCHANGE market speculators forced the pound to abandon the EXCHANGE RATE MECHANISM.

BLOCK TRADING
Trading in big blocks of shares. On the NEW YORK STOCK EXCHANGE any deal of more than 10,000 shares, or $1m-worth of bonds, is called a block trade. Such deals are usually carried out by financial institutions. Certain stockbrokers specialise in block trading.

The daily number of block trades is recorded and watched closely by market analysts. It gives an indication of how active financial institutions are vis-à-vis individual investors.

BLUE CHIP
The STOCK of a first-rate industrial company – ie, one with a long record of steadily rising PROFIT, and of uninterrupted DIVIDEND payments.

BLUE-SKY LAWS

Legislation passed by individual states in the USA regulating the sale of corporate securities in that state. The legislation is designed to protect investors from FRAUD.

Charles Blunt, brother of John Blunt, the leading fraudster in the South Sea Bubble, cut his throat in September 1720, the month the bubble burst. Contemporary press reports said he had committed suicide "upon some discontent".

BOND

An INTEREST-bearing instrument issued by governments, corporations and some other organisations. Bonds are sold to investors in order to raise CAPITAL and they may be bought and sold many times over in the SECONDARY MARKET before they are finally redeemed. Bonds are sold at a DISCOUNT (or PREMIUM) to their face value, such discount (or premium) reflecting the difference between the (fixed) interest rate on the bond's COUPON and the current market interest rate. (See also BEARER SECURITY and JUNK BOND.)

Gentlemen prefer bonds.
Andrew Mellon

BONUS ISSUE

See SCRIP ISSUE.

BOOK

The accounting record of a business, or of financial securities. Book-keeping is the maintaining of the ledgers and other books of record of a business, or of an ISSUE of securities. With every securities issue and SYNDICATED LOAN, one BANK (or brokerage firm) is selected to manage the book (for a fee). Today most book-keeping is done on computers.

BOOK RUNNER

The BANK or securities firm that is responsible for

the documentation and general management following the ISSUE of a SECURITY or a SYNDICATED LOAN.

BOOK VALUE
The value of a company's assets as expressed in its balance sheet. This can be less than the assets' market value since accounting convention may dictate that the assets be included in the accounts at their purchase price. INFLATION alone may well have ensured that this is less than the assets' current market value.

BOUGHT LEDGER
The department in a company that deals with its payments. It puts into effect the company's policy on CREDIT: how much to grant to its creditors, and over what period of time.

BOURSE
The continental European expression for STOCK EXCHANGE.

BRANCH
The retail outlet of a BANK; the shops around the country where it collects deposits, makes loans and arranges money-transmission services. Electronic banking (via ATMS etc) is increasingly making branches (and the people who work in them) redundant.

BRIDGING LOAN
A LOAN that spans the short period from now to the time when a more long-term credit FACILITY can be arranged.

Bridging loans are commonly used for house purchase (before a long-term MORTGAGE has been set up), and for financially distressed developing countries (see BANK FOR INTERNATIONAL SETTLEMENTS).

BROKER
An individual or a firm that buys and sells financial instruments on behalf of others. A broker is an AGENT who works for investors and financial institutions. His or her reward comes in the form of a

COMMISSION based on the value of the transactions that the broker undertakes. This gives the broker system an in-built incentive to CHURN clients' portfolios.

He's called a broker because after you deal with him you are.

Anon.

BUDGET

A plan (or estimate) of revenue and expenditure for a specific period in the future. In a balanced budget, revenue and expenditure are equal.

Budgets are necessary because income and expenditure do not occur at the same time. In large companies budgeting is an annual process, with future income and expenditure broken down into monthly (or even weekly) estimates.

A budget may take several months to prepare. It starts with an estimate of sales and income, then moves on to estimate the expenditure on materials, administration, production, research, distribution, and so on, that will be needed for that level of sales.

National budgeting is the process of doing this for a whole nation.

CAPITAL budgets are made up for periods in excess of one year. They include estimates of future capital expenditure, and of the borrowing required for it.

BUDGET ACCOUNT

See ACCOUNT.

BUILDING SOCIETY

A type of financial institution that grew up in the industrial towns of the UK in the nineteenth century (and from which to a large extent they took their names, such as Bradford, Burnley, Halifax, Leeds, Leicester). Building societies were designed initially to do little more than take in local short-term savings and put them out as long-term loans for house-purchase (mortgages). In recent years, however, they have been allowed to become much more competitive with banks. The banks have encroached on to their traditional MORTGAGE territory, and the societies have begun to offer money-transmission services and loans for purposes other than house purchase. Several of them have abandoned their MUTUAL status for full incorporation.

BULL

A person who expects the price of a SECURITY (or of a whole securities market) to rise. The opposite of a BEAR. Bulls will buy shares now expecting to be able to sell them later at a higher price. Bulls who are losing their nerve are known as stale bulls.

BULLDOG BOND

A bond denominated in sterling but issued by a non-British borrower.

BULLET

A LOAN on which all the PRINCIPAL is repaid in one go at the end of the period of the loan. During the life of the loan the borrower pays INTEREST only.

BUNDESBANK

Germany's CENTRAL BANK, housed in a modern block in a Frankfurt suburb since it had to leave its Berlin headquarters after the second world war, but due to return to Berlin. As central banks go, the Bundesbank is unusually independent of government, and is the zealous guardian of Germany's low-INFLATION economy. However, its purely national constitution has brought it into conflict with the increasingly pan-European responsibilities of the German government.

BUNNY BOND

A BOND where the investor has the option to receive INTEREST in CASH or in the form of more of the same bond.

BUY-BACK

An agreement in a sales CONTRACT whereby the

vendor agrees to buy back the property if certain conditions are (or are not) met within a certain period. For example, an agreement to buy back a house if the purchaser has to move on within a certain period of time; or an agreement to buy back a stake in a company if it fails to reach a pre-agreed level of PROFIT during its first year in new hands.

BUYER CREDIT
A medium- to long-term LOAN granted to a foreign buyer of exported goods. The loan is given by the exporter's BANK and usually carries the GUARANTEE of the exporter's national EXPORT CREDIT agency.

BUYER'S MARKET
A market in which there is a plentiful supply of commodities (or securities or whatever), and in which (as a consequence) prices are weak.

CALL

A demand made by a company on a shareholder to pay for shares that have been issued as PARTLY PAID.

CALL OPTION

A CONTRACT to buy a certain number of shares at a stated price (the STRIKE PRICE) within a specified period of time. A call option will be exercised when the SPOT PRICE goes above the strike price. If it is not exercised, the option expires at the end of the specified period of time.

CAMEL

An acronym for the five things that BANK supervisors look for most keenly when examining a bank.

1 CAPITAL adequacy.
2 Asset quality.
3 Management quality.
4 Earnings.
5 LIQUIDITY.

CAP

A ceiling imposed on the amount of INTEREST and/or CAPITAL that is to be repaid on a LOAN. With a US ADJUSTABLE RATE MORTGAGE there can be a number of different caps:

- annual adjustment caps which place a restriction on the amount of interest that can be paid in one year;
- a life-of-loan cap which places a ceiling on the amount of interest that can be paid on the loan throughout its life;
- a payment cap, which limits the amount of change in the monthly repayments from year to year.

CAPITAL

The money used to build a business. Capital is raised by issuing shares and long-term DEBT instruments. The balance of a company's ordinary shares, preference shares and long-term debt constitutes its capital structure. Together with its retained PROFIT, these make up the company's capital employed. The key relationship between debt and EQUITY is known as GEARING (or leverage in the USA).

For financial institutions, capital is a safety net against sudden losses arising from BAD DEBT, bad management, or skulduggery (see also WORKING CAPITAL).

CAPITAL ALLOWANCE

Part of the amount paid for capital equipment that can be set against income for the purposes of calculating a company's taxable PROFIT. The demand for capital equipment in an economy can thus be controlled to some extent by governments' fine-tuning of these allowances, both by their amount and by the things that they can be set against. For example, allowances might vary as to the period over which the capital expenditure can be set off (20% a year for five years) or by the percentage that can be set off (60% in year one, but no more).

CAPITAL EMPLOYED

The CAPITAL in use in a business. There is no universally agreed definition of what this includes, but it is usually taken to mean NET assets (that is, current assets plus fixed assets less current liabilities) plus bank loans and overdrafts.

CAPITAL FLIGHT

See FLIGHT CAPITAL.

CAPITAL GAIN

The PROFIT from the sale of a CAPITAL asset (such as a BOND or SHARE). In most countries capital gains are subject to special tax rules. In a few countries, however, capital gains are treated for tax purposes in the same way as income.

CAPITAL MARKET

Any market in those long-term financial instruments (like shares and bonds) that make up a company's CAPITAL.

C

Capital ratio

The ratio of a BANK's CAPITAL and RESERVES to its total assets. In most countries this is not allowed to exceed a prescribed ceiling.

Capitalisation

The attribution of a capital value to a stream of income. This value is the amount that would have to be invested now in order to produce a particular income stream in the future (see also MARKET CAPITALISATION).

In accounting the term means recording costs as assets rather than as expenses. For example, a company might captialise research and development costs.

In STOCK EXCHANGE parlance it is the aggregate market price of all a company's ORDINARY SHARES.

Captive

Refers to the practice of setting up insurance companies (or fund managers) inside large multinational groups for the express purpose of handling all the multinational's own insurance or fund management needs. A "captive" insurer or fund manager is expected to handle all of the group's business (and to be cheaper than buying the services from outside). But a captive may also seek business from other customers as well.

Carry back or carry forward

The capacity to shift tax advantages, or pension payment privileges, from one year into another, either back into a fiscal year that has ended, or forward into one that has not yet begun.

In God we trust. All others pay cash.
Anon.

Cash

Ready money; most obviously notes and coin, but also liquid assets that can be turned into notes and coin rapidly and without loss. The demand for cash varies throughout the year, being particularly strong, for example, in Christian countries at Christmas time.

CASH FLOW

The amount of money flowing through an organisation (or, indeed, an individual) in a given period. For a company, cash flow is the sum of its new borrowings plus money from any SHARE issues, plus its trading PROFIT, plus any DEPRECIATION. A company can be recording rising profits year-by-year while its CASH is ebbing away.

CASH MARKET

See SPOT PRICE.

CASH ON DELIVERY

Commonly known by its acronym COD, cash on delivery refers to goods or services that must be paid for in full at the time they are handed over to the buyer. The American term is collect on delivery.

CATS

See CERTIFICATE OF ACCRUAL ON TREASURY SECURITIES.

CBOE

See CHICAGO BOARD OF OPTIONS EXCHANGE.

CBOT

See CHICAGO BOARD OF TRADE.

CD

See CERTIFICATE OF DEPOSIT.

CEDEL

See CENTRALE DE LIVRAISON DE VALEURS MOBILIERES.

CENTRAL BANK

The institution at the hub of a nation's monetary and financial system. Each major developed country has one (see BUNDESBANK and FEDERAL RESERVE SYSTEM), but they do not all do the same things.

Central banks carry out some combination of five different functions.

1 They act as banker to the government.
2 They act as banker to commercial banks.
3 They supervise the banking system.
4 They print and issue the nation's currency.
5 They are the LENDER OF LAST RESORT, a back-stop that can print money in a severe financial crisis.

CENTRALE DE LIVRAISON DE VALEURS MOBILIERES
A computerised CLEARING HOUSE for Eurobonds and other international securities. Based in Luxembourg, Centrale de Livraison de Valeurs Mobilières (CEDEL) was founded in 1971, and is owned by a number of financial institutions. Its only real competitor is Euroclear, which began in 1968 and is based in Brussels.

CERTIFICATE OF ACCRUAL ON TREASURY SECURITIES
An American financial invention. Certificates of accrual on treasury securities (CATS) are US Treasury bonds that pay no INTEREST during their life (see ZERO-COUPON BOND). They are therefore sold at a deep DISCOUNT to their face value, and redeemed at their full face value on MATURITY.

CATS also stands for Computer Assisted Trading System, a piece of software developed by the Toronto Stock Exchange.

CERTIFICATE OF DEPOSIT
A certificate issued by a bank to indicate ownership of a large DEPOSIT (usually over $10,000). A certificate of deposit (CD) is a NEGOTIABLE INSTRUMENT and can be bought and sold on a SECONDARY MARKET between the time that it is issued and the time that it is redeemed.

CFTC
See COMMODITIES FUTURES TRADING COMMISSION.

CHARGE
There are at least two meanings.

1 Property pledged or taken as SECURITY for a LOAN, as in "the BUILDING SOCIETY that lent them the money to buy a home has a charge on the house".

2 The cost of goods or services, particularly of financial services; for example, BANK charges, the fees paid to banks by their customers for services. The basis for these charges is often opaque, and bank customers have only recently begun to demand clear statements of how their charges are calculated.

CHARGE CARD

A plastic card that allows its owner to buy goods before paying for them. Charge cards are often issued by department stores to their regular customers. The customers can then spend as much as they like in the store until the day each month on which they have to pay the outstanding debt charged to their card in full.

Some charge cards have a credit facility attached which allows the repayment to be spread over time. There is a fine distinction between a charge card and a TRAVEL AND ENTERTAINMENT CARD.

CHARTISM

The art of predicting future price movements of STOCK and other securities by looking at past price movements. Thus chartists spend their time examining charts which plot price movements over time. They look for recurring patterns (like a head and two shoulders), and on the basis of these patterns try to forecast future price movements. (See HEAD AND SHOULDERS.)

The popularity of chartism tends to be cyclical.

CHEQUE

A BILL OF EXCHANGE drawn on a BANK, and payable on demand. With the development of plastic cards and the growth of the AUTOMATED TELLER MACHINE, the demise of the cheque has long been predicted. But announcements of its death have been premature.

- A cheque is "stopped" when a bank refuses to clear it, that is, refuses to transfer the funds as requested (frequently because the funds are not there). The bank returns the cheque to the branch it came from.

- A post-dated cheque is one which has a future date on it, before which it cannot be cleared.
- A crossed cheque can only be credited to a payee's bank account; it cannot be paid in cash.
- A blank cheque is one where the amount to be paid is left blank, to be filled in by the payee.

(See also TRAVELLER'S CHEQUE and EUROCHEQUE.)

The cheque's in the post.
Everyman

CHEQUE CLEARING

A has an ACCOUNT at Bank X and B has an account at Bank Y. When A writes a CHEQUE to B it passes between Bank X and Y; the banks then clear it by debiting A's account and crediting B's.

Cheque clearing began in the 18th century coffee houses of London's Lombard Street where bank clerks would meet in order to exchange bundles of cheques among themselves.

CHICAGO BOARD OF OPTIONS EXCHANGE

The largest options market in the USA, and a subsidiary of the CHICAGO BOARD OF TRADE. The Chicago Board of Options Exchange (CBOE) was founded in 1973.

CHICAGO BOARD OF TRADE

The largest FUTURES exchange in the world. The Chicago Board of Trade (CBOT) and the CHICAGO MERCANTILE EXCHANGE between them handle about half of all the world's trading in futures. The CBOT is stronger in financial futures; the CME in commodities.

CHICAGO MERCANTILE EXCHANGE

Set up in 1919, the Chicago Mercantile Exchange

(CME) is a major CASH market and FUTURES market for the trading of commodities. It pioneered trading in livestock futures (pork bellies, and so on).

CHINESE WALL

A partition between two parts of a financial institution that are supposed to act independently of each other. Their independence is required in order to avoid conflicts of interest between different types of business. For example, a divide between the corporate finance side of an INVESTMENT BANK (involved in new SHARE issues) and its FUND MANAGEMENT side. Without separation, the fund managers might be tempted to buy the corporate financiers' new issues in order to help the bank sell something that was not going very well, rather than because they are a good investment for the fund.

Chinese walls need not be physical; but many institutions do put different parts of their business (where conflicts might arise) in different buildings.

CHURN

To trade excessively in the shares of a client's account, with the result that the BROKER makes a large amount of COMMISSION income (based on turnover). In the USA churning is illegal if it can be proved that the SHARE sales in question were largely inappropriate for the client.

CIRCULAR TRANSACTION

When two companies carry out reciprocal transactions in order to inflate each other's accounts artificially. For example, A sells B $1m of goods, and B immediately sells A $1m of the same goods. After the transaction nothing has changed except for the stated turnover of each company, which has become $1m higher than it would otherwise have been.

THE CITY

The name of that part of London that is roughly bounded by St Paul's Cathedral to the west and the Tower of London to the east. It is also the collective name of the many financial institutions in the area, as in "the City thinks that the RATE OF INTEREST is set to fall".

The City (also known as the Square Mile, which gives an approximate idea of its size) is home to many foreign banks and securities houses because London is the world's busiest international financial centre. They are there because traditionally banks had to be within easy walking distance of their supervisor, the Bank of England, which sits in the centre of the City.

If you want loyalty, get a dog.
City broker

CITY BANKS
The dozen large commercial banks that dominate the Japanese financial system. They not only lend vast amounts to Japanese industry (and not very much to Japanese consumers), but they are also intertwined in the large industrial/financial complexes (called *zaibatsu*) which many believe account for much of Japan's post-war economic success. City banks are very close to their industrial customers and able to wield great influence over them.

CLASS ACTION
A lawsuit brought about by individuals in their position as members of a class. For example, a legal action (alleging fraud, say) initiated by an individual shareholder on behalf of all shareholders.

CLEAN PRICE
A price for a bond which does not include any interest that may have accrued on it between the date of the last interest payment and the date of the price quotation. (See also DIRTY PRICE.)

CLEARING BANK
A type of commercial BANK in the UK with authority to clear cheques (see CHEQUE CLEARING).

CLEARING HOUSE

A firm or agency that handles the processes involved in transferring money or a SECURITY from one owner to another. A clearing house enables those institutions that use it to net off their credits and debits against each other at the end of each working day. They then need make only one payment transfer to each other per day.

CLOSED-END FUND

A fund which has a fixed number of shares. Investors who want to buy into the fund have to buy its shares in a SECONDARY MARKET. A closed-end fund is the opposite of an open-end fund (like a MUTUAL FUND) which simply issues new units every time a new investor wants to buy into the fund.

In the UK a closed-end fund is called an INVESTMENT TRUST.

CLOSING PRICE

The official STOCK-EXCHANGE price of a SHARE at the end of the exchange's trading day.

CME

See CHICAGO MERCANTILE EXCHANGE.

CMO

See COLLATERALISED MORTGAGE OBLIGATION.

COB

See COMMISSION DES OPERATIONS DE BOURSE.

COD

See CASH ON DELIVERY.

CO-FINANCING

A technique for bringing the international muscle of institutions such as the WORLD BANK and the Asian Development Bank together with the financial clout of commercial banks. Projects in developing countries are co-financed jointly by the international institution and a group of commercial banks.

Co-financing gives the banks the comfort of

knowing that borrowers rarely if ever default on loans from the World Bank *et al.* The World Bank benefits from the extra billions that commercial banks can bring to a negotiating table.

COLLATERAL

Property that is provided by a third party as SECURITY for a borrower, as in "my father let me use his house as collateral for a LOAN". The fine distinction between collateral (which is provided by a third party) and SECURITY (which is provided by the borrower) still exists in the UK. In the USA the two words are virtually indistinguishable.

COMEX

See COMMODITY EXCHANGE INC.

COMFORT LETTER

A letter required by US securities legislation. Written by an independent auditor, it guarantees that the information appearing in a PROSPECTUS has not altered materially in the time between the preparation of the prospectus and its distribution to the public.

COMMERCIAL PAPER

Short-term DEBT instruments issued by top-notch companies and banks. Born first in the US financial markets, commercial paper spread rapidly throughout Europe and the Far East during the 1980s.

Commercial paper has a maturity of 5–365 days (most frequently 30–90), and is issued in dollops that can be as small as $10,000 or as large as $1m. It is sold at a DISCOUNT to its face value, and is rarely INTEREST-bearing. When issued in the EUROMARKET, such instruments are known as Eurocommercial paper.

COMMISSION

The reward of an AGENT, usually expressed as a percentage of the sales that the agent generates on behalf of his or her client. In most industries there are accepted standard percentage commissions for different types of business. Any negotiation of commissions is done around these base points.

COMMISSION DES OPERATIONS DE BOURSE

The official watchdog of the Paris BOURSE. The Commission des Opérations de Bourse (COB) is a government agency that supervises new listings on the bourse, monitors takeovers and looks out for INSIDER DEALING. The COB's power and influence has grown in line with the rapid growth of the French STOCKMARKET.

COMMITMENT FEE

A payment made to a lender in return for the GUARANTEE of a LOAN (up to a certain size) as and when needed. The fee is usually a fraction of 1% of the amount committed.

COMMODITY

A raw material that is usually sold in bulk, and often on the floor of an exchange. Common commodities are grains, metals and certain foodstuffs (like pork bellies, orange juice and coffee). The most valuable commodities of all (by turnover) are oil and GOLD.

COMMODITY EXCHANGE INC.

A US commodities market founded in 1870. The Commodity Exchange Inc. (Comex) has markets in FUTURES and options as well as its traditional spot markets in metals such as GOLD, silver, copper and aluminium. Together with the London Metal Exchange, it dominates world trading in metals.

COMMODITIES FUTURES TRADING COMMISSION

The Commodities Futures Trading Commission (CFTC) was set up in 1979 by the US Congress to regulate US commodity FUTURES markets.

COMMUTATION

The exchange of part of a future pension for CASH now.

COMPENSATING BALANCE

An amount that a customer is asked to deposit with a BANK when the bank makes a LOAN to the customer. On the surface this sounds rather odd. Why borrow money from a bank simply in order to put it back into the bank?

The rationale for compensating balances lies in a time when there were strict limits on the RATE OF INTEREST that could be charged to lenders. Banks that wanted to charge more would charge the top legal rate and then insist that borrowers also deposit a certain amount (interest-free) with the bank. This free balance would compensate for the interest payments that the bank was unable to collect on the loan.

COMPLIANCE OFFICER

An employee of a securities firm who is appointed to make sure that the firm follows the (increasingly complex) rules laid down by financial-market regulators.

CONCERT PARTY

A group of investors who act together (and in secret) to try to gain control of a company. Each buys a small stake which, when combined, gives them control.

CONFLICT OF INTEREST

An occasion where the interests of a person or firm in one guise are in conflict with the interests of the person or firm in another guise. For example, a bank advising a company in its battle against a takeover will have a conflict of interest if it is also a shareholder in the bidding company. CHINESE WALLS are designed to reduce conflicts of interest.

CONSENSUS

The common name for the International Agreement for Guidelines on Officially Supported Export Credit. The consensus is an agreement between member countries of the OECD on how far they will go in subsidising the RATE OF INTEREST on loans to buyers of their country's exports. The minimum interest rates that they agree to permit vary according to whether the importing country is relatively rich, intermediate, or relatively poor.

CONSORTIUM BANK

A BANK owned by a group of other banks from a number of different countries. Consortium banks were popular in the 1970s when they were seen as a way to gain a toehold in the markets represented by all the other banks in the consortium. Many of these consortium arrangements have been disbanded because banks became confident enough to go into new markets on their own or decided that the markets were not sufficiently interesting.

CONSUMER CREDIT

A LOAN granted to enable someone to buy consumer goods like cars, washing machines, and so on. In many countries there are specific laws about consumer credit, designed to prevent the consumer from being exploited. In the USA at least 12 different government agencies are concerned in some way with ensuring that consumer credit is granted fairly.

CONTANGO

The situation where prices for future delivery of commodities are higher than for present delivery. This is the opposite of BACKWARDATION and is sometimes known as forwardation.

CONTRACT

In general, a legally binding agreement between two parties that one will supply goods or services to the other for a specified price.

A contract is also the unit in which options are traded, normally representing an OPTION on 1,000 shares of an underlying SECURITY.

In FUTURES, a contract is an agreement to buy or sell specific amounts of a COMMODITY in the future.

CONVERTIBLE

The capacity of one FINANCIAL INSTRUMENT to be

converted into another. The expression is usually applied to bonds or preference shares that can be converted into ordinary shares at a specified time, and at the request of the bondholder.

CORPORATE BOND
A BOND issued by a corporation.

CORRESPONDENT BANK
Before banks opened their own branches across the globe they used to manage their international business by setting up a network of loose relationships with other banks in different countries. These so-called correspondent banks provided services in their home market for the others in the network, and vice versa.

COST OF CAPITAL
An average of the costs of a company's various types of CAPITAL: ordinary shares, preference shares, debentures, bonds, loans, retained PROFIT, and so on. The cost of a LOAN is the INTEREST paid on it; the cost of a SHARE is the DIVIDEND. The tax treatment of these costs (interest and dividends) varies in such a way that it is usually more attractive for companies to borrow than to raise new EQUITY.

COUPON
A piece of paper attached to a BEARER SECURITY giving the bearer the right to the income (INTEREST or DIVIDEND) that comes with the security. To collect income due, the bearer must detach the coupon and present it to the paying AGENT of the issuer of the security.

The word "coupon" is also used to refer to the interest rate itself.

On October 29th 1929, Black Tuesday, 16.4m shares were traded on the New York Stock Exchange, a record that remained unbroken until 1968.

COVER
Funds to provide protection against loss (as in IN-

SURANCE cover), or to guarantee payment of a liability (as in DIVIDEND cover). Dividend cover refers to the number of times that a company's dividend payment can be covered by its total post-tax PROFIT (earnings).

CRASH

What happens when a STOCKMARKET falls unnaturally, and a lot of financial institutions go bust at the same time. The greatest crash of the 20th century occurred in 1929 in the USA. J.K. Galbraith, in his classic book *The Great Crash 1929*, attributed it to five main causes.

1 The poor distribution of income in American society. The top 5% of the population was reckoned to be receiving 33% of all personal income.
2 Bad corporate structure. The 1920s was a decade of stockmarket fraudsters and crooks who bled corporations of huge sums of money.
3 Bad banking structure. There were too many independent units, and the structure was such that the failure of one led to others collapsing in a domino effect.
4 The USA's foreign balance. There was a declining trade surplus for the first time in modern history.
5 The poor state of economic intelligence at the time. The government made decisions that were contrary to the best interests of the economy, but there was inadequate data on what actually was the state of the economy.

Between September 3rd 1929 and July 2nd 1932 the Dow Jones Industrial Average index of the New York stockmarket fell from 381.7 to 41.2, its lowest figure ever, wiping out over $70 billion.

CREDIT

A LOAN, or the ability to raise a loan, as in "he bought the washing machine on credit" and "her credit at the bank is good".

CREDIT CARD

A rectangular piece of plastic that empowers its

owner to buy goods and services, and to buy them on CREDIT. The use of credit cards has grown rapidly in recent years.

Most credit cards are issued by banks and retailers. The credit card business is dominated by two powerful brand names, Visa and Mastercard. These are marketing organisations to which the banks that issue cards are affiliated. (See also CHARGE CARD.)

CREDIT LINE

A CREDIT limit agreed between a customer and a BANK, which the customer can draw upon as and when required.

CREDIT NOTE

A written message informing a customer that his or her account with a supplier has been credited (and by how much). Credit notes are frequently used when a customer returns goods as being below standard, or when there has been a short shipment.

CREDIT RATING

A formal assessment of a company's creditworthiness, and of its capacity to meet payment schedules on time. A credit rating is often obtained by a trader dealing with a new customer for the first time. It may come from the client's bankers or existing suppliers, or from one of the specialist agencies (like Dun & Bradstreet) that provide such ratings, for a fee.

After the fall of the Austrian bank Creditanstalt in Vienna in May 1931, there was a run on German banks by investor/speculators who did not know the difference between Austria and Germany.
Charles Kindleberger, *Manias, Panics and Crashes*

CREDIT UNION

An organisation in which a group of people with a common bond get together to pool their savings. They then lend those savings to each other. Credit unions are popular in the USA where they are non-PROFIT-making organisations.

CREST

The London Stock Exchange's electronic share settlement system, first introduced in 1996. All companies whose shares are handled by CREST (which includes the shares of all those companies which make up the Footsie, London's leading stockmarket index) have fully electronic registers of shareholders. Paper share certificates are gradually disappearing, and may soon come to have much the same curiosity value as 19th century railway bonds.

Unlike its non-electronic predecessors, CREST is not owned by the London Stock Exchange. This is one of many indications of the declining influence of traditional stock exchanges.

CROSS DEFAULT

A condition that may be attached to a debt or security saying that if the borrower/issuer defaults on any of its other debts or securities, then that automatically counts as a default in respect of the debt or security which contains the cross-default clause. The lender then has the right to pursue repayment as if the borrower/issuer were in default on his debt or security.

CUM DIV

The opposite of EX-DIV: a SHARE being sold together with the right to a DIVIDEND that has been declared but not yet paid. Similarly, cum rights is a share that is being sold together with the right to take up a new offer of shares.

CURRENT ACCOUNT

See ACCOUNT.

CURRENT RATIO

The ratio of a business's current liabilities to its current assets.

- Current assets = CASH, bank deposits and

other items that can be quickly turned into cash.
- Current liabilities = SHORT-TERM loans and trade CREDIT.
- Current assets minus current liabilities = WORKING CAPITAL. (See also CAPITAL EMPLOYED.)

The current ratio is used as a guide to a company's solvency. It has only limited use in comparing companies across industries, however. The appropriate current ratio for a company depends on the industrial sector that it belongs to, and on the normal terms of trade in that industry. These terms can vary greatly.

CUSHION BOND

A BOND that can be retired early, that can be called in before it reaches MATURITY. There is a stated price (the CALL price) at which such bonds can be called, and this inevitably holds down the SECONDARY-MARKET price of cushion bonds. However, it also helps to stabilise the price of the bonds in times of turbulent INTEREST rates.

CUSTODIAN

Somebody (usually a BANK or a lawyer) who holds an investor's securities on behalf of the investor. A custodian handles everything that arises from ownership of those securities, such as the collection of income, voting at meetings, exercising rights, and so on.

DEBENTURE

A long-term DEBT instrument, often secured on the general creditworthiness of the issuer rather than on any specific asset. When a company is being liquidated, debenture holders have a right to the company's leftovers before ordinary bondholders.

DEBIT CARD

A piece of plastic much like a CREDIT CARD, except that it gives the holder no CREDIT. A debit card is passed through an electronic reading device at a point of sale and thus debits the holder's bank ACCOUNT automatically (and immediately) with the value of the sale.

DEBT

An obligation of one person to pay something (usually money) to another.

Never run into debt, not if you can find anything else to run into.

Josh Billings

DEBT SERVICE RATIO

The ratio of a country's annual repayments on its foreign DEBT to the value of its annual HARD-CURRENCY export earnings. The ratio is used as a (first-stab) guide to a country's creditworthiness.

For many Latin American countries in the 1980s the ratio was well over 100%. All their hard-currency export earnings (and more) went to service their debt to foreign banks and governments.

You can't cheat an honest man.

W.C. Fields

DEFAULT

Failure to repay a LOAN according to the terms of a CONTRACT. Once a borrower is in default there are a number of legal moves that a lender can make in order to try and recover the money, or to get hold of any underlying SECURITY backing the loan.

DEFEASANCE
The placing of assets, like CASH and treasury bills, in trust by the issuer of a BOND. All the INTEREST and PRINCIPAL due on the bond are subsequently repaid out of these assets, by the TRUSTEE.

DELIVERY
The transfer of title to a FINANCIAL INSTRUMENT from one owner to another. Hence delivery date, delivery month, and so on, the time when delivery is to be made.

In COMMODITY markets there are three classes of delivery.

- **Current delivery.** Delivery in the current calendar month.
- **Nearby delivery.** Delivery in the next calendar month.
- **Distant delivery.** Delivery in a month that is further away.

DEMATERIALISE
In finance, the word is used to refer to the process of transferring into electronic form something that was previously recorded in paper form. Thus it can be said that shares are gradually being "dematerialised" as they are increasingly stored electronically (see CREST). It can also be said that banks themselves are dematerialising as their branches become fewer and fewer, and their dealings increasingly take place "on line" (see DIRECT).

DEPOSIT
There are several meanings.

1 Money left as SECURITY before receipt of a service, such as a tenant might give a landlord before moving into a furnished property, or a telephone company might demand before connecting a line for a new customer.
2 Natural resources found underground, as in "South Africa's rich mineral deposits".
3 Money left with a BANK for safe-keeping. Such deposits come in many different forms.

- **Demand deposit.** Money that can be withdrawn on demand or without notice. Also known as sight deposits, and usually non-interest-bearing.
- **Savings deposit.** A sort of piggy bank account, designed for regular savings that are rarely withdrawn. It pays interest, but at below market rates.
- **Time deposit.** A deposit that can be withdrawn only after a specified period of time; for example, a three-month deposit, or a six-month deposit. These deposits pay interest at close-to-market rates, and are also known as fixed deposits.

DEPOSIT PROTECTION

An INSURANCE scheme into which banks pay a PREMIUM in order to protect depositors against loss should the BANK go bust. Such schemes usually give limited protection, covering small deposits up to a certain fixed amount and insuring larger deposits only up to that amount. This tempts big depositors to spread their money around a number of institutions in order to get the maximum insurance COVER.

The main argument against these schemes is that they give badly run institutions a competitive advantage, because small depositors become indifferent to the institution that they leave their money with. (See FEDERAL DEPOSIT INSURANCE CORPORATION.)

DEPRECIATION

The effect of the passage of time (wear and tear or technical obsolescence, for example) on the value of assets; recognition that the value of an asset at one end of an accounting year is different from its value at the other end. Accountants deduct an amount from annual PROFIT to take account of depreciation.

Accountants use three ways of calculating depreciation for the purposes of a company's books.

- **The straight-line method.** This takes an estimated scrap value of the asset at the end of its life, and subtracts this from its original cost. This is then divided by the number of years of useful life that the asset is expected to have.

- **The reducing balance method.** This takes a fixed percentage of the value of the asset last year and sets that aside out of PROFIT; and so on, every year.
- **The inflation-adjusted method.** This tries to take account of the fact (ignored by other methods) that the cost of replacing an asset at the end of its life will usually be greater (if only because of INFLATION) than the original cost of the asset. It sets aside, out of profit each year, an amount adjusted for the rate of inflation during the year.

All these methods ignore the fact that in a fast-changing technological world most assets are unlikely to be replaced with anything like themselves. In some cases (with computers, for example) the cost of replacement may be considerably less than the original cost, inflation notwithstanding.

Roger Babson did badly in the 1929 depression by being right too soon. He got his clients out of the market in 1928.

Charles Kindleberger, *Manias, Panics and Crashes*

DEREGULATION
The process of removing legal or quasi-legal restrictions on the types of business done, or on the prices charged, within a particular industry. The aim of most deregulation is to increase competition by increasing the freedom of players in the industry.

In recent years a number of industries (including airlines, telecoms, banking and stockbroking) have been deregulated around the world. In the USA the removal of INTEREST-rate ceilings (called Regulation Q) was one example of price deregulation; in the UK the introduction of DUAL CAPACITY in the STOCKMARKET was an example of non-price deregulation.

Regulation has not always arisen as a whim of despotic governments. It is often there to protect consumers. For example, if airlines were allowed to compete too fiercely safety standards might fall, with fatal consequences. Likewise, if banks compete too fiercely their deposits may be put at risk.

DERIVATIVES

General term for financial assets that are "derived" from other financial assets – for example, an option to buy a treasury bond: the option (one financial asset) is derived from the bond (the other financial asset). Regulators worry that markets for derivatives treacherously undermine markets for the original underlying assets.

DEVALUATION

A sudden downward jerk in the value of a currency vis-à-vis other currencies. Devaluations occur when a country's costs have risen faster than those of its competitors, and when its exports are no longer competitive in price.

Devaluations are exacerbated by the activity of speculators in the FOREIGN-EXCHANGE markets. They buy and sell vast quantities of currencies in anticipation of a devaluation.

Devaluations can result in huge relative changes in a currency's value; 10% overnight, for example. This can wipe out any ordinary exporter's PROFIT at a stroke, which is one good reason why exporters prefer to work within a framework of relatively fixed exchange rates.

DILUTION

When a company issues more shares, and sells them for less than their market price, the value of each existing SHARE is diluted. The total value of the company is being divided into a larger number of little pieces (ie, shares). Hence the value that attaches to each little piece gets smaller.

Companies sometimes talk about their fully diluted EARNINGS PER SHARE. This refers to the earnings per share when all shares are included: ordinary shares plus any convertible securities (that is, convertible into shares), and all warrants and STOCK options.

DIRECT

The general word for the way in which financial services that are sold by telephone rather than face-to-face by an agent (in insurance) or over the counter (in banking) – as in "direct insurance", or "direct banking". There has been rapid growth in the direct selling of financial services in recent years, and this has enabled many firms to cut out middle men. In insurance, for example, the commissions of traditional agents have been greatly reduced. Banks have been left looking for ways to cut their branches, and their staff.

DIRECT DEBIT

An instruction from a BANK's customer asking the bank regularly to debit his or her ACCOUNT with the amount demanded by a named creditor. Direct debits are designed to make it easy to pay regular but varying bills (like those of utilities). For many years they were resisted by bank customers, who were nervous of the way that they took control of their finances out of their hands.

DIRTY PRICE

A price for a bond which includes the amount of interest that has accrued on the bond since the date of the last interest payment. (See also CLEAN PRICE.)

DISCOUNT

There are two meanings.

1 The verb means to sell at a reduced price.
2 The noun refers to the reduction in price itself. A CASH discount is a reduction in price given to someone who pays immediately for goods, in cash or in a cash equivalent. A trade discount is a reduction in price given to someone who is in the same trade as the vendor. For example, by a wholesaler

of garments to the owner of a fashion boutique.

When a bill is sold at a discount to its face value, the discount represents the INTEREST forgone between the time of the sale and the date that the bill matures.

DISCOUNT RATE

In general, the RATE OF INTEREST represented by the sale of a FINANCIAL INSTRUMENT for less than the PRINCIPAL repayment due on MATURITY. In particular, the interest rate at which a CENTRAL BANK discounts government bonds and other first-class DEBT instruments to commercial banks; or the rate at which central banks lend to commercial banks, using the bills as COLLATERAL.

DISCOUNT WINDOW

A facility provided by central banks whereby commercial banks can lodge their surplus RESERVES or top up their reserves against the SECURITY of their top-quality assets.

DISCRETIONARY ACCOUNT

An ACCOUNT that an investor has with a BROKER which gives the broker discretion to act on behalf of the investor without consultation. This discretion may apply only within certain pre-agreed limits.

DISINTERMEDIATION

The exclusion of financial intermediaries from the process of allocating savings. This can happen in several ways.

- A company may choose to raise EQUITY, or issue bonds, directly in the financial markets rather than borrow from its BANK.
- A government may choose to raise revenue by issuing attractive savings bonds that are sold directly to the public, rather than by the more traditional way of selling treasury bonds to banks.

To some extent disintermediation is a function of the economic cycle. Market rates tend to move ahead of bank INTEREST rates. So when rates are rising, investors prefer to put their money directly into the markets, and borrowers are happy to pay marginally more for easy access to this money. When rates are falling, bank rates lag behind market rates. Investors then switch their money out of the markets and into financial institutions.

In the longer term, with the creation of a wider variety of more sophisticated financial market instruments, the opportunities for disintermediation will increase.

DIVIDEND

That part of the earnings of a company that is distributed to its shareholders. Payment of a dividend is not automatic. It is decided upon by the company, and declared by its board of directors. In the USA this usually takes place every three months; in most other countries it occurs every six months.

Dividends on preference shares are paid at a fixed rate; but on all other shares (in theory) they vary. Many companies, however, find that the RISK from cutting their dividend from one year to the next is considerable. Their SHARE price might fall, and the cost of raising new CAPITAL rise as a consequence.

Hence companies go to great lengths to maintain (and if possible increase) their dividends year on year. This has at least two important consequences.

- CASH FLOW for other purposes (such as further capital investment) is often squeezed in order to pay dividends. Some companies go so far as to increase their bank borrowing in order to maintain their dividend.
- Shareholders (supposedly RISK-taking investors) become like the holders of treasury bonds, secure in their expectation of a steady future income (see GILTS).

DIVIDEND COVER

The number of times that a company's annual dividends can be divided into its annual earnings.

Thus if a company's after-tax earnings in a year are $20m, and it pays out $2.5m in dividends that year, its dividend cover is eight.

This is similar to the dividend payout ratio, a concept popular in the USA. The dividend payout ratio is the percentage of the company's earnings paid to shareholders in CASH. With old mature industries this tends to be high (and the dividend cover, therefore, low). But for young growing businesses that need CAPITAL for reinvestment, it tends to be low (and the dividend cover high).

DOCUMENTARY CREDIT

A method of financing trade. Banks provide the buyer of goods with credit to pay the exporter on the strength of documents which prove that the buyer has proper title to the goods. This is useful when documents reach the buyer more quickly than the goods themselves.

DOUBLE-TAXATION AGREEMENT

It is a fundamental principle of tax law in most nations that the same income should not be taxed twice. In consequence, there is a network of agreements between pairs of nations that seek to avoid taxing income in one country when it has already been taxed in another.

This applies in particular to income that arises in one country but is then remitted to a resident in another.

Double taxation can also occur when income passes from one taxable entity (like a corporation) to another (like a shareholder). Attempts to reduce the double taxation of dividends (paid out of a company's taxed income to taxable individuals) have been less widespread than the attempts to eliminate the taxation of the same income in two fiscal jurisdictions.

DOW JONES INDEXES

Dow Jones, the company which publishes the WALL STREET JOURNAL, also gives its name to the most famous STOCKMARKET index in the world. The

Dow Jones Industrial average (instituted in October 1896) is a closely watched INDEX based on the average prices of a selection of about 30 companies quoted on the NEW YORK STOCK EXCHANGE. It gives an indication of the rate and direction in which the stockmarket as a whole is moving.

There are other less widely reported Dow Jones indexes. They include an index of public utility SHARE prices, and an index of railway company share prices.

The record fall in the Dow Jones Industrial average on a single day was 508 points (22.6%) on October 19th 1987 (Black Monday). The record rise was 186.8 points, two days later.

DOWNGRADE
A reduction in the RATING of a company, or of its DEBT securities.

DRAWDOWN
Making use of funds that have been made available under a bank FACILITY.

DUAL CAPACITY
The ability of the same financial institution to be both STOCKBROKER (that is AGENT) and stock JOBBER or MARKET MAKER (that is principal). (See also BIG BANG.) In any business, being both an agent and a principal inevitably leads to a potential CONFLICT OF INTEREST. In stockbroking, for example, it presents opportunities to put good deals (retrospectively) on an institution's own books, while placing loss-making deals on the books of clients.

DUE DATE
The date when an INTEREST or PRINCIPAL payment becomes due.

DUE DILIGENCE
The thorough search of a business done either by the potential manager of a new ISSUE of the company's securities; or by a company intending

to take over the business.

The purpose of due diligence (normally carried out by accountants or financial experts) is to check that the company's sales figures and general performance are as it claims they are. In the case of a possible takeover this is a delicate exercise. The company carrying out the due diligence has made no binding commitment to buy the business that it is examining. Should it back out of the negotiations it may have obtained commercially sensitive information for nothing. On the other hand, only rarely can a vendor hope to sell a business without giving the purchaser some chance to look at the books in advance of a sale.

DUTCH AUCTION

An auction in which the auctioneer's prices fall rather than rise. In such an auction, the first person to bid wins whatever it is the auctioneer is selling. The system is used in the Dutch flower markets and also, occasionally, as a method of selling securities.

EARNINGS PER SHARE

A measure of the total return earned by a company on its ORDINARY SHARE capital: the NET profit of the company divided by the number of ordinary shares in issue. Net PROFIT is the gross profit (receipts minus costs) less DEPRECIATION, INTEREST charges, PREFERENCE SHARE payments and tax.

A company that makes a net profit of $10m and has 2m shares outstanding has earnings per share (EPS) of $5. EPS is seen as a particularly helpful guide to a company's past, present and future performance. (See also DILUTION.)

EASDAQ

A pan-European stockmarket designed for high-growth companies and modelled on America's NASDAQ. EASDAQ is based in Brussels and is independent of any national European stockmarket. It is authorised by the Belgian Banking and Finance Commission.

Much like NASDAQ, EASDAQ provides the platform for a screen-based market in high-tech stocks. It is owned by about 90 financial intermediaries (both American and European), and began operations in November 1996.

EBRD

See EUROPEAN BANK FOR RECONSTRUCTION AND DEVELOPMENT.

E-COMMERCE

That commerce which is carried out electronically; in particular, any commerce carried out over the Internet. (Compare with E-mail.)

The development of E-COMMERCE has been restrained by the difficulty in finding secure methods of payment over the Internet. Customers have yet to be convinced that their credit-card details will not become accessible to any casual hacker after they have been keyed into the Net.

ECONOMIC AND MONETARY UNION

The process of bringing together the currencies and monetary policies of the member states of the

European Union so that the whole EU bloc lives and works with a single currency (to be called the Euro), and is governed by a single central bank (the EUROPEAN MONETARY INSTITUTE).

The timetable for EMU, laid down in the Maastricht Treaty which was signed by all the EU member states, is meant to begin in earnest in 1999. The Treaty also established certain criteria which member states must meet if they are to participate fully in EMU. The criteria include:

- that government debt be less than 60% of GDP;
- that the general government deficit be less than 3% of GDP;
- that inflation be less than 3.1%;
- that government bond yields be less than 8.5%.

Ecu

See EUROPEAN CURRENCY UNIT.

EFTPOS

See ELECTRONIC FUNDS TRANSFER AT THE POINT OF SALE

Egibi

Possibly the first recorded BANK in history. Mr Egibi, the bank's founder, lived in Damascus in the latter part of the reign of the Babylonian king Sennacherib (705–681BC). A stone tablet recording the bank's first loan is in the British Museum.

EIB

See EUROPEAN INVESTMENT BANK.

ELECTRONIC FUNDS TRANSFER AT THE POINT OF SALE

A way of paying for shopping electronically, commonly known by its acronym EFTPOS. A plastic card gives the retailer electronic access to a customer's bank ACCOUNT. The account is debited immediately and automatically with the cost of the goods. (See also DEBIT CARD.)

The disadvantage of electronic payment systems from the customer's point of view is that they are immediate. There are none of those helpful 3–4 day delays between the time that an old-fashioned CHEQUE is handed over and the time it is debited from the payer's account. With EFTPOS, moreover, any mistakes have to be rectified after the payment has been made.

EMERGING MARKET
A stockmarket in a fast-developing economy (like Taiwan or India) that has little history of domestic capital markets. In the late 1980s and early 1990s some of these emerging markets grew at a very rapid rate. Their growth was fuelled by an increasing supply of new shares – from local privatisations and from the flotation of old-established family firms – and by an increasing demand from western investors for stocks whose price would increase more rapidly than those in their own stagnant domestic markets.

As western stockmarkets rebounded in the mid-1990s, the growth of emerging markets slowed down.

EMPLOYEE STOCK OWNERSHIP PLAN
An American scheme designed to encourage employees to buy STOCK in the companies that they work for. There are tax advantages to such schemes; companies can deduct for tax purposes any dividends paid to employees under them.

EMS
See EUROPEAN MONETARY SYSTEM.

EMU
See ECONOMIC AND MONETARY UNION.

ENDORSEMENT
The signature on the back of a CHEQUE (or similar FINANCIAL INSTRUMENT) which transfers ownership of the instrument from the signatory to the bearer. A bearer instrument, such as an open cheque, does not need endorsement.

ENDOWMENT MORTGAGE

A MORTGAGE linked with a life-insurance policy. During the life of the mortgage, the mortgagee pays only INTEREST on it. However, he or she also pays premiums on a policy which matures at the same time as the end of the loan. The capital sum assured by the policy should cover the PRINCIPAL that has to be repaid on the mortgage.

EPS

See EARNINGS PER SHARE.

EQUITY

The ownership interest of shareholders in a company, as in "he launched a new company last year, and he has 20% of the equity". On the company's balance sheet, equity is what is left over when all the company's external liabilities have been deducted from its assets.

Equity has also come to mean the excess or surplus value of a capital asset over and above the DEBT still owed on the asset. For example, the amount by which the market value of the securities in a customer's MARGIN ACCOUNT with a BROKER exceed the debt still due on the account; or the amount by which the market value of a house exceeds the MORTGAGE on the house.

ERM

See EXCHANGE RATE MECHANISM.

The highest tax demand in history was for $336m on the estate of Howard Hughes.

ESCROW ACCOUNT

A bank ACCOUNT kept by a third party on behalf of two others who are (usually) in dispute about its rightful ownership. The disputing parties try to set out conditions under which they will agree to let the money be released. When these conditions have been met, the third party releases the funds.

ESOP

See EMPLOYEE STOCK OWNERSHIP PLAN.

EURO

The name of the single European currency that under the terms of the Maastricht Treaty is to be introduced into the member states of the European Union in stages from January 1999. According to the plan, for the first three years of its life the currency will be used mostly by banks in dealings among themselves. Then, over a six month period in the year 2002, national currencies will be withdrawn, to be replaced by the Euro.

EUROBOND

A BOND issued by a company or a government, with two peculiar characteristics.

- It is issued in a market other than that of its currency of denomination.
- The banks that issue it sell it internationally, not just in one domestic market.

Thus, if Germany's Deutsche Bank were to issue a dollar-denominated bond for France's Aerospatiale, and to sell it around the world, it would be a Eurobond. If it were to sell the bond only in Germany it would be a foreign bond. Eurobonds are peculiar in having no home base whose government can support them should their market collapse.

EUROMARKET

A market in financial instruments held in countries other than the one which issued the currency in which they are denominated: for example, the market for dollar deposits in Europe (that is Eurodollars), or the market for Deutschmarks (Eurodeutschmarks) in the USA.

EURO.NM

An association of European stockmarkets that are designed for smaller companies. The members are the second-tier markets in Amsterdam, Brussels,

Frankfurt (the Neuer Markt, launched in 1997), and Paris (the Nouveau Marché launched in 1996).

The exchanges banded together partly in order to defend themselves from competition from London's AIM, which has ambitions to be a Europe-wide capital market for smaller companies, and from EASDAQ.

EUROPEAN BANK FOR RECONSTRUCTION AND DEVELOPMENT

A special institution set up to channel aid to eastern Europe. Although created largely on the initiative of the European Community, the European Bank for Reconstruction and Development (EBRD) has 40 member countries. It opened its doors for business (in London) in 1991 with plans to grant 40% of its loans to the public sectors of eastern Europe, and 60% to the growing private sectors.

EUROPEAN CURRENCY UNIT

An artificial creation based on a basket of European currencies. The European Currency Unit (or ecu) has been gradually expanding its uses since it was invented by the European Community at the end of 1978. Its purpose then was to act as a reserve asset and as a means of settlement in the EUROPEAN MONETARY SYSTEM. Now it appears in several guises.

- Deposits and loans (particularly mortgages) denominated in ecus are offered by a number of banks.
- Many of the European Commission's payments to subcontractors are denominated in ecus.
- The ecu is actively traded in the FOREIGN-EXCHANGE market.
- There is a substantial ecu BOND market.
- The EUROPEAN INVESTMENT BANK denominates its accounts in ecus.

The composition of the ecu is subject to review every five years.

(See also EURO and SPECIAL DRAWING RIGHTS.)

EUROPEAN INVESTMENT BANK

A BANK created in 1957 by the Treaty of Rome (the treaty which first established the existence of what has become the European Union). The European Investment Bank (EIB) acts as a development bank for Europe, using its good name to borrow cheaply on international capital markets, and then lending those (cheap) funds to borrowers in the EU and associate member states.

Most EIB loans are for terms of 7–12 years. The bank has certain priorities. It favours lending for the following.

- Depressed EC areas like Portugal and Greece.
- The development of European technology.
- Infrastructure projects that involve more than one EU member country, like the Channel Tunnel.
- Projects that further a particular interest of the EU.

EUROPEAN MONETARY INSTITUTE (EMI)

The forerunner of the single European central bank that will be made necessary by EMU and the single European currency. The EMI was established in 1994 and is based in Frankfurt. Its function is to strengthen monetary co-ordination among member states and set up the infrastructure necessary for the proper functioning of a single European monetary policy and a single European currency.

The European Central Bank (ECB) will operate as a sort of Euro-Fed (ie, a European version of the FEDERAL RESERVE SYSTEM). There will be a European System of Central Banks (ESCB) which will consist of the ECB and the central banks of the EU member states that are participating in EMU.

EUROPEAN MONETARY SYSTEM

A scheme to manage the way in which European currencies' exchange rates move against each other. The European Monetary System (EMS) started on March 13th 1979 as the successor to the snake, the first concerted attempt to dampen fluctuations in exchange rates since the dollar had been allowed to float freely in 1971.

There are three mechanisms at the heart of the EMS.

- The EXCHANGE RATE MECHANISM.
- Accounting and settlement mechanisms in which central banks swap some of their RESERVES for ecus (a mere accounting device). They then carry out transactions among themselves in these ecus. (See EUROPEAN CURRENCY UNIT.)
- CREDIT mechanisms which enable central banks to obtain loans from other member states' central banks when (and if) they need to bolster their currency – in order to keep it within the limits of the ERM, for example.

The controversial Maastricht Treaty laid out plans to take the EMS several giant steps further. It provides a schedule to implement European monetary union through a system of permanently interlocked exchange rates and a single monetary policy. It is designed to lead ultimately to the adoption of a single European currency.

EXCHANGE CONTROL

The method by which governments attempt to control the flow of currency in and out of their country; both foreign currencies and the government's own currency. The UK maintained strict exchange controls for a number of years after the second world war. It abolished them only in 1979. France abolished its last controls even later.

EXCHANGE RATE MECHANISM

A central part of the EUROPEAN MONETARY SYSTEM. The Exchange Rate Mechanism (ERM) is an agreement to maintain exchange rates among member states of the European Community within agreed limits, thus guaranteeing a degree of monetary stability within the boundaries of the EU.

EX-DIV

An indication given next to a quoted SHARE price

showing that the price does not include payment of a DIVIDEND that has been declared by the company but not yet paid. Ex-div means that the dividend is to be paid to the previous owner of the share.

Likewise, ex-rights means that a share price does not include a recent RIGHTS ISSUE. The rights may either remain with the previous owner, or be sold separately. Ex-new is similar to ex-rights: the purchaser is not buying a right to new shares. (See also CUM DIV.)

EXERCISE
Making use of a right that is available under the terms of a CONTRACT; for example, exercising an OPTION to purchase a SHARE at a certain price within a certain time.

The right in question may also be the conversion of a convertible SECURITY into a share.

EXERCISE PRICE
See STRIKE PRICE.

EXPIRY DATE
The last day on which a particular right (to buy shares at an advantageous price, for example) can be exercised.

EXPORT CREDIT
A LOAN to an exporter to tide it over the period between the time when its goods are sent abroad and the time when it receives payment for them. With exports of large capital goods that time may be anything up to several years.

EXTERNAL FUNDS
Sources of funds that are available to a company from outside the company itself. Thus the proceeds of a BOND issue or a bank LOAN are external funds; retained PROFIT is an internal source of funds (see INTERNAL FUNDS).

FACILITY

A banking service (such as an OVERDRAFT facility) that is made available to customers for their use as and when they please. A facility letter is a letter from a bank confirming in writing the details of a specific LOAN that has been made available.

FACTORING

The business of collecting someone else's debts on their behalf. A company sells its receivables (that is, its unpaid invoices) to a factor (often the subsidiary of a BANK) at a DISCOUNT. The factor then sets out to collect the money owed. Its PROFIT comes when it has collected more than the discounted price that it paid for the debts.

The company that sells its debts to a factor gets a helpful boost to its CASH FLOW.

Factoring may also include any or all of the following.

- Maintaining the company's sales ledger.
- Managing the company's CREDIT control; that is, making sure that it does not give customers excessively long periods to repay.
- The actual collection of unpaid DEBT.
- INSURANCE cover against BAD DEBT.

Factoring is divided into disclosed and undisclosed. Disclosed factoring, in which the factor lets the debtors know that it is collecting payments on behalf of the client, is increasingly common. Undisclosed factoring (also known as confidential invoice discounting) allows the client to conceal the fact that it has employed a factor.

FANNIE MAE

See FEDERAL NATIONAL MORTGAGE ASSOCIATION.

A London banker called Henry Fauntleroy who forged notes in order to keep his bank afloat, was executed for his crime in 1824.

FDIC
See FEDERAL DEPOSIT INSURANCE CORPORATION.

FED FUNDS RATE
The rate at which US banks lend their surplus RESERVES to each other overnight. The reserves are generally non-INTEREST bearing deposits held with the FEDERAL RESERVE SYSTEM. Banks hold them in order to meet their required CAPITAL RATIO.

The fed funds rate is taken as a particularly sensitive indicator of the way in which US interest rates in general are moving.

FEDERAL DEPOSIT INSURANCE CORPORATION
The USA's DEPOSIT PROTECTION fund, established in 1933 in the depths of the Great Depression. The Federal Deposit Insurance Corporation (FDIC) has changed its name to the Bank Insurance Fund (BIF), and now insures all deposits up to $100,000 at banks that take out INSURANCE cover with it.

A similar institution does a similar job for the USA's troubled savings and loan associations. Formerly called the Federal Savings and Loan Insurance Corporation (FSLIC), it too has changed its name – to the Savings Association Insurance Fund (SAIF).

FEDERAL HOME LOAN MORTGAGE CORPORATION
Commonly known as Freddie Mac, a semi-public US body which guarantees mortgages and finances them by issuing securities. It is largely owned by savings banks, and is similar to the FEDERAL NATIONAL MORTGAGE ASSOCIATION.

FEDERAL NATIONAL MORTGAGE ASSOCIATION
Commonly known as Fannie Mae, a company created by the US Congress to support the secondary MORTGAGE market. It buys and sells mortgages, and is financed by the issue of bonds. At times it has owned as many as 10% of all US mortgages. Its shares are quoted on the NEW YORK STOCK EXCHANGE.

FEDERAL RESERVE SYSTEM

Commonly known as the Fed, the CENTRAL BANK of the USA and thus the guardian of the value of the dollar. The Fed is both the regulator of banks in the USA and the controller of the money supply. It works through 12 regional federal reserve banks spread across the country. Each is owned by banks in its area, and each has nine directors serving a three-year term of office.

At the pinnacle of the system is the Federal Reserve Board, consisting of seven governors and based in Washington, DC. Each governor is appointed by the US president for a 14-year term, a long time for people who are rarely young when they start the job.

The Fed carries out the usual monetary and FOREIGN-EXCHANGE responsibilities of a central bank. In addition, it is the supervisor of US bank holding companies. In practice, it keeps an eye on all US banks, for whom it is the lender of last resort.

FIDUCIARY DEPOSIT

A Swiss speciality in which a BANK takes a DEPOSIT and lends it on to someone else, entirely at the depositor's own RISK. One of the big benefits for the bank is that the deposit remains off its balance sheet (so it does not have to set aside expensive RESERVES), yet the bank still makes a return on the transaction. The advantage for the depositor is a higher RATE OF INTEREST and the veil of Swiss secrecy.

Most fiduciary deposits are simply passed on to other banks and become straightforward Euro-currency deposits.

A financier is a pawnbroker with imagination.
Sir Arthur Wing Pinero

FINANCIAL CENTRE

Any place in which, for historical or fiscal reasons, more than an average amount of financial business is transacted. Centres can range from the big and indisputable (like London) to the small and ambitious (like the Cayman Islands).

FINANCIAL INSTRUMENT

Documentary evidence of the ownership of a financial asset; for example, a BILL OF EXCHANGE, CERTIFICATE OF DEPOSIT, government BOND, SHARE, STOCK, and so on.

FINANCIAL INTERMEDIARY

Any individual or institution that mediates between savers (that is, sources of funds) and borrowers (that is, users of funds). The chain from original source to ultimate use can be a long one, with many intermediaries along the way.

FINANCIAL TIMES

A daily financial newspaper printed on pink paper. It is the bible of the European financial community in the same way as the WALL STREET JOURNAL is for the United States. The *Financial Times* is owned by the Pearson Group which also owns half of *The Economist*.

The Financial Times *was founded by Horatio Bottomley, a particularly audacious swindler. Bottomley was also a member of Parliament, a job which he interspersed with being bankrupt, founding the* Hackney Hansard, *and going on trial several times for fraud. He eventually spent five years in jail.*

FINANCIAL YEAR

The 12-month period covered by a company's accounts. On occasions, a financial year can be a period of more or less than 12 months. For example, when a company wants to change the ending of its financial year from (say) inconvenient May to more convenient December, it will have to have a financial year of either seven months or of 19 months (7 + 12).

FIXED RATE

A rate of interest that does not change before the

maturity of the financial instrument to which it attaches. (See also VARIABLE RATE.)

FIXING
The setting of the GOLD price in London twice a day – at 10.30am and at about 3pm – by a number of big gold dealers.

FLIGHT CAPITAL
Money that rushes out of a country when political or economic uncertainty undermines people's faith in the currency's ability to maintain its value. Such money tends to head for stable places like Geneva and Miami, and for stable currencies like the Deutschmark and the dollar.

FLIP-FLOP BOND
A BOND that can be turned into another type of DEBT instrument at the investor's discretion, and can then equally easily be flipped back into the original form of investment.

FLOAT
There are two meanings.

1 The number of securities in an ISSUE that are free to be traded; that is, securities that are not held by investors who are unlikely or unable to sell them.
2 Money that arises in the accounts of banks from cheques in the process of being cleared.

FLOATING CHARGE
SECURITY given by a borrower to a lender that floats over all the borrower's assets. Thus if the borrower fails to repay the LOAN, the lender can claim any of the borrower's assets, up to the value of the loan.

FLOATING RATE
A RATE OF INTEREST that changes with the cost of funds.

FLOATING RATE NOTE
A BOND with a COUPON whose rate varies in line

with a market RATE OF INTEREST. Floating rate notes (FRNS) appeal particularly to borrowers who expect interest rates to fall. At such a time borrowers do not want to be locked into paying the fixed rates that are found on traditional bonds.

FLOOR
There are two meanings.

1 A minimum RATE OF INTEREST on a FLOATING RATE NOTE.
2 The place in a STOCK EXCHANGE where trading actually takes place (or used to).

FLOTATION
The launch of a new BOND or EQUITY issue on to a CAPITAL MARKET. On all markets there are complicated rules governing the way in which flotations must take place. Observance of the rules is ensured by regulators such as the SECURITIES AND EXCHANGE COMMISSION in the USA, and the COMMISSION DES OPERATIONS DE BOURSE in France. The rules (most of them designed to protect investors from fraud) add considerably to the cost of flotation. (See also INITIAL PUBLIC OFFERING.)

FOOTSIE
See FT-SE 100.

FORCED SAVINGS
Savings that accrue without the consumer making a conscious decision to save. This can happen in all sorts of ways: because governments levy taxes which go towards paying old-age pensions, for example; or because certain expenditure is prohibited, as when restrictions are imposed on foreign travel.

FORECASTING
The human instinct to try and predict the future is found everywhere, particularly in things financial. Any degree of certainty about the future that is not widely known promises huge gains to those who do know it.

FOREIGN BOND

A BOND denominated in a currency foreign to the issuer, and sold in the domestic market of the currency of issue. Thus a Swiss franc bond issued by a Japanese company and sold in Switzerland is a foreign bond on the Swiss market. (See also EUROBOND.)

FOREIGN EXCHANGE

The means whereby payments are made between one country and another. The foreign-exchange (forex) markets are among the biggest markets of any kind in the world, and dealers in them have shown that they can spoil the best-laid plans of ministers for their currency's exchange rate.

Huge sums of money cross the exchanges every day, much of it in search of short-term gain (even as short as overnight). Its effect on rates is at odds with the continual desire of industry and government to see stability in forex markets.

FORFAITING

Also known as à forfait, the business of discounting a FINANCIAL INSTRUMENT that is being used to finance the export of capital goods. Banks buy the instruments at a DISCOUNT, and then trade them.

The forfait market grew up in Switzerland, where it concentrated on buying east–west trade debts; but its name became increasingly Anglicised (from à forfait to forfaiting) as the market shifted to London in the 1980s.

Crime breeds in the gaps between opportunities and aspirations.
Graffito

FORGERY

A counterfeit coin, note or document that tries to pass as something that it is not. Forgeries often involve the copying of other people's signatures.

To make forgery as difficult as possible, the printing of notes has become a highly specialised task that involves the use of a number of sophisticated technical devices.

FORWARD CONTRACT

An agreement to buy a specified quantity of a COMMODITY or currency at some specified future time and place. A forward contract in the FOREIGN-EXCHANGE market might involve an agreement to buy £100,000-worth of three-month sterling for dollars; that is, to pay now (in dollars) for the delivery of £100,000 in three months' time.

The exchange rate to be paid for this sterling will reflect market expectations about the appreciation or DEPRECIATION of sterling against the dollar over the next three months. A premium over the spot rate will indicate expectations of a sterling appreciation; a DISCOUNT will indicate an expected depreciation.

FORWARD COVER

The process of covering future payments or receipts, either by buying now (in the FUTURES markets) the currency that is required for the payment; or by selling now a receipt that is due in the future.

This is particularly valuable in volatile FOREIGN-EXCHANGE markets where fluctuations in rates can wipe out an ordinary business's PROFIT (and more) in less time than it takes to print an invoice.

It is estimated that the average company in the USA loses between 2% and 5% of its gross turnover in fraud.

FRAUD

An act of deception aimed at gaining financial benefit illegally, at the expense of others. Fraud can be the result of many different kinds of deception, from lying in documents to back up a new ISSUE of securities, to false accounting in a company's annual reports, to pretending to be a registered BROKER, to simply forging notes.

FREDDIE MAC
See FEDERAL HOME LOAN MORTGAGE CORPORATION.

FRN
See FLOATING RATE NOTE.

FT-SE 100
The STOCK index introduced on January 1st 1984 by the FINANCIAL TIMES and the London STOCK EXCHANGE, known affectionately as FOOTSIE. FOOTSIE is a computerised index of 100 big UK companies. It was designed to fill a gap between the FT ordinary share index (started in 1935) which contained a mere 30 companies, and the FT all-share index which contained hundreds and was calculated infrequently.

FOOTSIE has now replaced the FT ordinary share index and become by far the most popular index of the London market. The first stock-index options and futures to be traded in London were based on the FOOTSIE.

The INDEX started life at a level of 1,000. The lowest it has ever reached was 986.9 on July 23rd 1984.

The greatest rise in the Footsie index in a single day was of 142.2 points on October 21st 1987 (7.9%); the greatest fall was of 278.3 points on the day before, October 20th (13.4%).

FUND MANAGEMENT
The process of managing other people's money with the aim of gaining a certain return on it. Big institutions, like pension funds and INSURANCE companies, spend much of their time managing the funds placed with them by thousands of small savers. Other firms specialise in managing funds that have been created by others – for example, a company's in-house pension fund.

FUNGIBLE
The quality of those things (like notes and coins) where any one single specimen is indistinguish-

able from any other. A person owed $1 does not bother which particular dollar note he or she receives, even if it is frayed at the edges. Anything to be used as money (be it cowrie shells, beads or GOLD pieces) has to be fungible.

FUTURES

Contracts to buy something in the future at a price agreed in the present. First developed in agricultural COMMODITY markets, like those for orange juice and pork bellies, futures then spread into financial markets. There are now futures in bank deposits, government bonds and STOCKMARKET indexes.

There has been fierce competition between different financial centres to set up the world's leading futures markets. Traditional centres have not had it all their own way. In the USA Chicago has given New York a run for its money; in Europe Paris's MATIF is fiercely competitive with London's LIFFE; and in the Far East Singapore is a more lively centre than Hong Kong.

GEARING

The indebtedness of a company expressed as a percentage of its EQUITY capital, referred to in the USA as leverage. A highly leveraged company is one with a lot of loans compared with its equity. (See also LEVERAGED BUY-OUT.)

GENERAL POLICY

An INSURANCE policy that gets around a trader's need to insure every single shipment separately. The trader and the insurer agree in advance on COVER up to a certain ceiling. The trader then merely advises the insurer on the nature and value of shipments when they are made and until (in total) they reach the ceiling.

GILTS

Short for gilt-edged SECURITY, a British term for those securities that are as good as GOLD; usually reserved exclusively for government bonds. Top-notch STOCK is usually referred to as BLUE CHIP.

GINNIE MAE

See GOVERNMENT NATIONAL MORTGAGE ASSOCIATION.

GIRO

A payment system organised by a group of banks, or by postal authorities. It enables institutions to make payments among themselves without shuffling CASH perpetually from one to another. A giro system transfers funds among accounts which the participating institutions hold at the giro's central CLEARING HOUSE.

GLASS-STEAGALL ACT

A law put forward by Senator Carter Glass and Representative Henry Steagall in 1933, a milestone in US banking legislation. The law prevents any commercial BANK in the USA from underwriting or dealing in securities. Securities business is left as the exclusive preserve of INVESTMENT BANKS.

This strict divide was created in the wake of financial scandals in the late 1920s and early 1930s. A number of banks had used depositors' money to support the price of securities that they were underwriting, sometimes with disastrous consequences for depositors. Today, however, Mr Glass and Mr Steagall's dividing line looks very frayed.

The act also authorised the first bank deposit INSURANCE scheme.

GLOBAL CUSTODY
A service for the worldwide safekeeping and settlement of securities. A small number of banks have managed to establish very profitable global custody businesses.

GLOBAL MARKET
A market for goods or services that attracts buyers from all over the world. The idea that there might be global markets for a very wide range of products and services (from Mars bars to mortgages) was first popularised in the 1980s.

However, many financial markets were global for many years before that.

- Customers of banks in London and New York come from all over the globe in search of trade finance facilities.
- LLOYD'S of London insures risks (especially those at sea) all over the world.
- Hard commodities (metals) and soft commodities (agricultural goods) have been bought and sold at COMMODITY exchanges in the major financial centres by buyers and sellers from all over the planet for at least a century.

GOLD
The precious metal that individuals most like to hoard when they feel uncertain about the value of money. Central banks also like to hold some of their nation's RESERVES in gold, to the tune of about 950m oz. The biggest store of the yellow metal is believed to be 80ft below the streets of Manhattan.

For much of the nineteenth century the UK had a monetary system that was based on gold (the so-called Gold Standard). Notes and coin were freely

convertible into their worth in gold by the CENTRAL
BANK, and gold was exported and imported freely
to settle accounts between the central banks of different nations. The Gold Standard was abandoned
in 1914 at the outbreak of the first world war.

One of the problems with using gold for such a
purpose was that the growth in world trade was
restricted by the world's ability to produce more
gold.

> *The value of the yellow metal, originally chosen
> as money because it tickled the fancy of savages,
> is clearly a chancy and irrelevant thing on which
> to base the value of our money and the stability
> of our industrial system.*
>
> D. H. Robertston, *Money* (1928)

GOLD CARD

Any plastic card (either a CREDIT CARD or a TRAVEL
AND ENTERTAINMENT CARD) which offers a number of
services in addition to those available from the
basic card. Gold cards are aimed at high earners
who are also high spenders; most require applicants to have a minimum income.

GOLDEN HANDCUFFS

A generous employment CONTRACT which per-
suades managers to stay with a company when
they might otherwise have thought of leaving; for
example, when the company comes under new
ownership.

> *F. Ross Johnson, once chief executive of RJR
> Nabisco, received a golden handshake of $53.8m
> on his departure in 1989. Eight years later
> Michael Ovitz, once president of Walt Disney,
> received "severance pay" of more than $100
> million after 16 months with the company – the
> largest pay-off in history.*

GOLDEN HANDSHAKE

A generous payment to employees to persuade

them to leave a company without making a fuss, even if they have not completed their CONTRACT. Senior managers in the past have been known to write the terms of their own golden handshake.

GOLDEN SHARE
A SHARE with special voting rights that give it peculiar power vis-à-vis other shares. The term applies particularly to shares retained by a government after PRIVATISATION. If a government wishes to sell off a company in a sensitive industry (defence, say), and yet retain control it can hold on to a golden share. This might give it the right (for example) to veto any takeover bid.

GOLDEN WEEK
An unusually short working week on the Tokyo STOCK EXCHANGE which straddles two long holiday weekends.

GOVERNMENT NATIONAL MORTGAGE ASSOCIATION
Commonly known as Ginnie Mae, a US quasi-government institution designed to support the housing market. It buys mortgages, bundles them together, insures them and then issues securities backed by them. These securities, which carry a government GUARANTEE, have been popular with American investors.

Well, fancy giving money to the government!
Might as well have put it down the drain.
Fancy giving money to the government.
Nobody will see the stuff again.
A. P. Herbert

GOVERNMENTS
In the USA a distinction is sometimes made between governments and government securities. Governments are securities (like treasury bills, bonds or notes) that are issued by the central government. They are backed by "the full faith and credit" of the US government, which means that all

its powers to tax or to borrow can be called upon to repay INTEREST or PRINCIPAL on the LOAN.

Government securities, on the other hand, are securities issued by US government agencies such as the Federal Land Bank. While these securities are usually highly rated, they do not have the full faith and credit of the US government behind them.

GRACE PERIOD
The time between the granting of a LOAN and the first repayment of PRINCIPAL. It is also a period in many loan or INSURANCE contracts during which cancellation of the CONTRACT will not occur automatically, even if a repayment is well overdue.

GREENBACK
Slang for the world's favourite currency: the dollar. The expression arose because the back of the USA's paper notes is green.

GREENMAIL
Common practice in the USA in the merger-mad 1980s. Somebody buys a large chunk of shares in a company and threatens to make a hostile takeover for the company. To buy him off the company buys back the shares at a much higher price than the greenmailer paid for them.

So disgusted were ordinary Americans with this practice that they passed legislation which imposed an onerous tax on any PROFIT made from greenmail.

GRESHAM'S LAW
One of the oldest laws in economics, named after Sir Thomas Gresham, financial adviser to Queen Elizabeth I of England in the sixteenth century. He noted that when a currency has been debased and a new one is introduced to replace it, the new one will be hoarded (and thus taken out of circulation) while the old one will continue to be used for transactions (to be got rid of). Hence Gresham's Law: that bad money drives out good.

GREY MARKET
Trading in shares in advance of the official start of

dealings. Shares are traded in the grey market before they have been allocated to investors. They are traded on a basis of "when issued", denoted by the letters WI.

GROUP ACCOUNTS

The combination within one balance sheet, and one PROFIT and loss account, of the reports of a number of interrelated companies (a group). A group usually consists of a parent company (the holding company) and a number of subsidiaries.

Group accounts eliminate intra-group transactions. Somebody looking only at the isolated accounts of a subsidiary might be misled if (say) most of the company's reported sales are to other companies in the group. In group accounts all such sales are netted out.

GROUP INSURANCE

INSURANCE obtained by an individual as a member of a group rather than as a single individual. For instance, an insurance company might offer favourable car-insurance terms to the over-50s (as a group), on the grounds that they drive more carefully and are less prone to accidents than the population as a whole.

GROWTH STOCK

A company SHARE that has shown faster than average growth in earnings in recent years, and that is expected to continue to do so over the next few years. Such shares do not usually pay much DIVIDEND, since the companies involved need all their earnings for reinvestment in order to feed further growth. Investors have to look to CAPITAL GAIN for their PROFIT.

GUARANTEE

An undertaking by a third party to be responsible for a liability (a LOAN from a BANK, for instance) should the party to the liability be unable or unwilling to meet the liability on time. To be legally binding, a guarantee must be in writing.

A guarantee differs from an indemnity in the

nature of the undertaking. With an indemnity the guarantor takes on responsibility in his or her own right. With a guarantee the guarantor takes on COLLATERAL responsibility; that is, the same degree of responsibility as the person he or she is guaranteeing. Should the guaranteed person die, then so does the guarantor's responsibility.

HAMMERING

An old expression for the failure of a London STOCK EXCHANGE member firm. An employee of the exchange would hammer for silence on the floor before making an announcement of a member firm's troubles.

In the USA hammering has come to refer to intense selling pressure on a market, when investors believe that prices are too high.

HANG SENG INDEX

The main INDEX of the Hong Kong STOCKMARKET.

HARD CURRENCY

A currency that people want to possess, and in which they are happy to denominate international transactions. Hard currencies are more in demand than soft currencies, and so they tend to appreciate in value against other currencies. The hardest major currency in recent years has been the Deutschmark; before that it was the Swiss franc, and before that the US dollar.

HEAD AND SHOULDERS

A recurring pattern on charts that plot market prices over time. A head and shoulders occurs when prices move up (the left hand arm), then stabilise briefly before moving up again (the left shoulder and the head). At the top of the head they move down to the right, pause again briefly on the right shoulder, before sliding steeply down the right arm.

Serious students of such charts maintain that a head and shoulders has great predictive value. It can be quite easily spotted by the time it has reached the right shoulder, by which time it is clearly flashing signals to sell. (See also CHARTISM.)

HEDGE

Something that reduces the RISK of loss from future price movements. In a time of high INFLATION, property is the traditional hedge. GOLD too is a popular hedge, but it has not been a reliable store of value in recent years. FUTURES and options provide opportunities for investors in financial markets to hedge their risks.

A perfect hedge is one which completely eliminates the risk of future loss (thereby also completely eliminating the chance of future gain).

HIRE PURCHASE

A means of paying for high-value consumer goods, like cars or televisions. At the point-of-sale the goods that the consumer wants to buy are sold to a financial institution. The institution then rents them to the consumer. After the consumer has made a (pre-arranged) number of regular payments and paid a small service fee, the goods become his or her property.

A number of specialised financial institutions provide this service. The RATE OF INTEREST they charge is usually higher than that on an ordinary bank LOAN.

HISTORIC COST

The cost of something on the day that it was purchased; its original cost, as opposed to its REPLACEMENT COST, or its INFLATION-adjusted cost. Accountants like historic cost because it gives them a real figure to play with. It is not very helpful, however, to say in a company's accounts that the value of its premises is the historic cost that was originally paid for them (which may be 100 years ago). This bears little relation to what it will cost to replace them today, or to their value in the market.

In the USA historic cost is known as historical cost.

HOLDING COMPANY

A company set up to hold shares in other companies. (See GROUP ACCOUNTS).

HOME BANKING

Banking done at home by individuals via the telephone or a television or computer screen, a little box (the modem) and a number of telephone lines.

HOT MONEY

Highly mobile CAPITAL that flows to wherever it finds the highest rate of return for a given level of RISK. Hot money has no long-term allegiance to any particular investment, so it flows back and forth across exchanges and can cause wild fluctuations in exchange rates. Such fluctuations have become more and more exaggerated in recent years as exchange controls have been removed, and as DEREGULATION has freed money to go where it wants.

> *There is perhaps no record of a bank fraud extant of which the perpetrator was not honest yesterday.*
>
> J.S. Gibbons, Bank of New York, 1857

HURDLE RATE

That RATE OF RETURN which a business has to achieve in order to justify its existence. The hurdle rate may be the rate of interest on government bonds – on the grounds that this is the least that investors can expect to get from an alternative investment. But it may be more demanding – for example, the return on equity (ROE) obtained by rivals in the same industry.

IBF

International Banking Facility, a special type of "offshore" organisation that has been permitted in the United States since 1981. IBFs are only allowed to carry out large financial transactions, and then only with non-residents. But those transactions are free from the reserve requirements imposed on domestic financial institutions (see Reserves), and in many cases they are also free from state and local taxes.

Tokyo followed suit in 1986 with the JOM (Japanese Offshore Market) where the restrictions are slightly more onerous than in New York.

IMF

See INTERNATIONAL MONETARY FUND.

IMPACT DAY

The day when details of a new ISSUE of securities are announced.

INCOME STATEMENT

See PROFIT AND LOSS ACCOUNT.

IN THE MONEY

A CALL OPTION is said to be in the money when it has a STRIKE PRICE below the current price of the underlying COMMODITY or SECURITY on which the option has been written. Likewise when a PUT OPTION has a strike price above the current price it is said to be in the money.

INDEMNITY

See GUARANTEE.

INDEX

A statistical average of the prices of a number of things. The things may be consumer goods (as in the consumer price index), or they may be stocks and shares, as in STOCKMARKET indexes like the DOW JONES or the FT-SE 100.

Some stockmarket indexes reflect a narrow part of the whole market (averaging the SHARE price of 30 BLUE-CHIP corporations, for example); others try to reflect the whole market by averaging most of the shares quoted on it. Yet others include stocks from only one industry or sector (an index of utilities or of mining stocks, for example).

An index is a useful way of seeing to what extent, and in what direction, prices are moving over time.

INDEX FUND

A MUTUAL FUND which invests in a PORTFOLIO of shares that matches identically the constituents of a well-known STOCKMARKET index. Hence changes in the value of the fund mirror changes in the INDEX itself.

INDEX-LINKED

The linking of the redemption value (and sometimes even the interest) of a security or loan to a general price index (for example, the index of retail prices). This is done in order to protect the value of the security or loan from the ravages of inflation. Whatever interest is paid after the indexing is the "real" rate of interest on the loan or security.

INDIVIDUAL RETIREMENT ACCOUNT

A special fund, set up under US tax law, into which an individual can put a certain amount of money each year, tax-free, towards his or her pension. Lump sum payments received on retirement or redundancy can also be placed into an individual retirement account (IRA), tax-free, within a certain time period.

When a pension is paid out of an IRA, the beneficiary pays tax on it like any other income. Thus the IRA is a means to defer tax payments rather than a way of avoiding them altogether.

INFLATION

A systematic rise in the price of goods and services over time. Economists differ in their views of what causes inflation. There are two basic theories.

- **Cost push.** That increases in the cost of the factors of production are the main cause. This includes the price of imported raw materials and any rise in property rents. Most importantly, it includes rises in wage costs. Hence employers argue that any wage increase above the rate of inflation is itself inflationary.
- **Demand pull.** That consumers are demanding more than is being produced, and thus pushing up prices. They can only do this if the amount of money in the economy exceeds the growth in production plus the rate of inflation.

One theory focuses anti-inflationary efforts on keeping down wage demands; the other on controlling the nation's MONEY SUPPLY.

Inflation undesirably redistributes wealth and income, hitting hardest those on fixed incomes and benefiting most those heavily in DEBT. It also undermines the basis for calculating value. It is not in itself, however, necessarily a deterrent to growth. Many developing countries have combined high growth rates with high inflation.

The highest rate of inflation recorded in recent times was not that in Germany in the 1930s, but in Hungary in 1946 where the 1931 gold pengo was valued at 130m trillion (1.3×10 to the power 20) paper pengos.
Guinness Book of Records

INITIAL PUBLIC OFFERING
A company's first offering of shares to the general public. An initial public offering (IPO) is frequently a traumatic experience for the company and its founders. They are often making the ISSUE in order to cash in on their creation, but they are rarely prepared for the public scrutiny that it involves.

INSIDER DEALING
Dealing in shares with the benefit of inside informa-

tion; that is, information not yet known to the general public. In some countries insider dealing is a crime, but it is a difficult crime to prove. How do you show that somebody found something out before he did a deal, and not after the deal was done?

INSTALMENT CREDIT

A LOAN that is repaid over a period in regular, equal instalments. Such loans are most often used to finance consumer purchases, but they are also sometimes used in trade finance.

Instalment credit differs from HIRE PURCHASE. In hire purchase, consumers hire the goods until they have paid off the loan; with instalment credit they own the goods throughout the time that they are paying off the loan.

---

*Wealthy people miss one of life's greatest thrills –
paying the last instalment.*

Anon.

INSTITUTIONAL INVESTOR

An institution (such as an INSURANCE company, PENSION FUND or INVESTMENT TRUST) that makes substantial investments by gathering together the small savings of others, and acting collectively on their behalf.

In recent years individuals' savings have been increasingly channelled through these institutions, and they have come to have great influence in most financial markets. In the UK, for example, such institutions now hold more than 70% of all quoted securities.

The institutions are stronger in Anglo-Saxon economies where pensions are more frequently funded by accumulated private-sector savings. In Mediterranean countries, for example, pensions are more often funded on a pay-as-you-go basis: the young pay for the pensions of the old as and when they are due.

INSURANCE

A CONTRACT between two parties (the insurer and

the insured) in which the insurer (usually an insurance company) agrees to reimburse the insured for clearly defined losses. It does so in return for the payment of a PREMIUM. In essence, this is a method of transferring RISK from an individual to a larger group (the group of all those who are paying premiums to the insurer).

There are two main types of insurance.

- **Casualty.** Here there is no certainty that the thing insured against will occur. Common forms of casualty insurance are against accidents (in cars or boats or planes), against damage to buildings, and against sickness.
- **Life.** Here the thing insured against is certain to occur: the death of the insured. The only uncertainty is when. This sort of insurance is usually referred to as life assurance because the event is assured of happening.

Life assurance is traditionally sold directly by sales people to customers in their homes; casualty insurance is usually sold by insurance agents who match a customer's needs with insurance policies available on the market. Agents are widely used because the terms and conditions of different policies vary greatly and can be extremely complicated.

Insurance is like fun.
The older you get the more it costs.
Frank Hubbard

INTERBANK MARKET

A financial market in which banks deal with each other; a crucial part of any efficient financial system. Banks that get more deposits from their customers than requests for loans need a market in which to sell their surplus deposits to those in the opposite position. For example, banks in leafy suburban districts tend to gather more deposits than banks in the heart of grimy industrial areas.

INTEREST

There are two meanings.

1 The price of money over time. (See RATE OF INTEREST, ANNUALISED PERCENTAGE RATE, COUPON, DISCOUNT RATE, INTERNAL RATE OF RETURN, NEGATIVE INTEREST, VARIABLE RATE and YIELD.)

If the rate of interest is 8% per annum, then for someone to borrow $100 for a whole year will cost them $8, when calculated as simple interest. Compound interest involves paying interest on the PRINCIPAL and on accrued interest as well. Hence if interest is due every six months, but is only paid annually, the interest due would be 8% on $100 for six months (that is $4) plus 8% on $104 for the next six months.

2 Somebody's share in property; as in "she had a 50% interest in the house".

Waiting necessarily commands a price.
Gustav Cassel

INTEREST COVERAGE RATIO

The number of times that a company's annual INTEREST payments can be divided into its NET operating income. An indicator of how sure the company's creditors can be of repayment.

INTEREST-ONLY LOAN

A LOAN on which only INTEREST is paid at regular intervals until the loan matures, at which time the full amount of the PRINCIPAL is repaid. This differs from the case where interest and principal are repaid throughout the life of the loan in a series of regular repayments.

INTERIM DIVIDEND

Part of a company's DIVIDEND paid at intervals during the year. Interim dividends may be paid after six months or (sometimes with US companies) every quarter. They are rarely paid more frequently.

INTERNAL FUNDS

Companies have two sources that they can turn to when in need of money.

- EXTERNAL FUNDS from banks, financial markets and shareholders.
- Internal funds from the fruits of their own labour; cash retained in the business and not distributed to shareholders.

Companies in different countries have traditionally had very different proportions of external to internal funds.

INTERNAL RATE OF RETURN

That RATE OF INTEREST which would discount the flow of revenue generated by an investment, so that the NET PRESENT VALUE of the flow is equal to the capital sum invested.

The internal rate of return (IRR) is much used in appraising whether investment proposals are financially viable. It does not always give the same result as using NET PRESENT VALUE as a yardstick. One project can have a higher net present value than another, yet have a lower IRR.

INTERNATIONAL BANK FOR RECONSTRUCTION AND DEVELOPMENT

See WORLD BANK.

INTERNATIONAL MONETARY FUND

An institution set up as part of the landmark Bretton Woods agreement of 1944. The role of the International Monetary Fund (IMF) was to oversee the system of fixed exchange rates which prevailed at the time.

As fixed exchange-rate systems have broken down, the IMF has found new roles for itself. It was deeply involved in sorting out the developing-country DEBT crisis of the early 1980s, imposing economic conditions on nations before agreeing to new loans and to the RESCHEDULING of old ones.

Headquartered in Washington, DC, the IMF has over 140 member countries. Originally confined to the capitalist West, they now include many of the newly converted states of eastern Europe.

Each country pays a membership fee (its quota) which is related to the size of its economy. Members can then borrow up to 25% of their quota at will; any more and they have to accept certain conditions from the IMF on their economic performance. The managing director of the IMF is traditionally a European and the deputy managing director an American.

INTERNATIONAL SECURITIES MARKET ASSOCIATION

Founded in 1969 in Zürich, the ISMA was originally called the Association of International Bond Dealers (AIBD) but changed its name in 1991. It is a loosely knit club whose 820 member firms from over 40 countries deal in and underwrite international bonds. ISMA issues rules and regulations, and supervises the activities of its members.

INTRODUCTION

A way of introducing a company to a STOCKMARKET. No new shares are issued, but existing shares (which may have been in the hands of a small number of founding managers, or the members of one family) are spread around and sold more widely.

INVERSE YIELD CURVE

In the normal structure of INTEREST rates, the rate for long-term FINANCIAL INSTRUMENTS is higher than that for SHORT-TERM ones. Plot this as a graph (rates on the vertical axis, MATURITY on the horizontal axis) and the curve slopes upwards from the bottom left-hand corner to the top right.

In circumstances, for example, where there are strong expectations that a currently high INFLATION rate will soon fall rapidly, this curve can slope the other way; the longer the maturity, the lower the rates. Plotting this on a graph is said to produce an inverse yield curve.

INVESTMENT BANK

A BANK whose main business is raising money for companies (or similar organisations) by marketing new public issues of the organisation's securities, or by placing private DEBT instruments with lenders. In the UK such a bank is generally called a MERCHANT BANK.

INVESTMENT CLUB
A group of private investors who agree to pool their funds and manage the funds themselves. The advantages of such a club are that investors have greater control over their investments, and they save the management fees of a professional fund manager.

Investment clubs are increasingly popular in the United States among communities of retired people.

INVESTMENT GRADE
In the United States certain financial institutions are not allowed to invest in bonds that have a rating lower than a certain grade from the major credit-rating agencies (a BBB rating from Standard & Poor, for example). If a bond is eligible to be bought by these institutions then it is said to be of investment grade. Bonds that have a rating below investment grade are known as junk bonds.

INVESTMENT TRUST
An institution that issues shares to investors, and reinvests their money in a diversified PORTFOLIO of securities. An investment trust thus gives the small investor the benefit of diversification without the enormous transaction cost usually associated with it.

For some reason investment trusts often trade at a substantial DISCOUNT to the value of the shares in their portfolios. This leaves them vulnerable to takeover by an ASSET STRIPPER.

INVESTOR RELATIONS
The job of keeping investors in a company informed about what the company is up to. Until recently, investor relations was merely one part of public relations. But as the demands (and the significance) of shareholders have increased, compa-

nies have split the job of keeping them happy from the job of keeping others informed about the company's activities.

INVISIBLES

Traded items that never see the inside of a container, but which earn foreign currency nevertheless. Services like banking, INSURANCE and tourism make up the bulk of a nation's invisible trade. Some countries have a big surplus in invisibles because they are especially attractive to tourists or to bankers.

Increasingly, however, the distinction between visible and invisible trade is becoming blurred. When Ford sells a (visible) car outside the USA its price includes a lot of (invisible) services, such as the company's R&D facilities, financing, and so on. And when tourists go home they (usually) take a lot of visible items with them in their luggage.

IPO

See INITIAL PUBLIC OFFERING.

IRA

See INDIVIDUAL RETIREMENT ACCOUNT.

ISIN

International Securities Identification Number, a 12-digit alpha-numeric code that uniquely identifies each issue of securities. Drawn up under the auspices of the International Organisation for Standardisation (ISO) and published as ISO 6166, an ISIN should appear on every security and COUPON.

ISLAMIC BANKING

Banking run according to the laws of the Koran. Essentially, these forbid the payment of interest. So Islamic banks do not have depositors to whom they pay interest; rather they have partners who share in the profits of the businesses into which their money is channelled by the banks. Likewise, businesses which receive money from Islamic banks do not pay the bank interest; they share with it their profits, again as if they were partners.

Islamic banking sounds straightforward in theory, but it has proved difficult to put into practice. It is only now becoming widely established in the Muslim world.

ISMA
See INTERNATIONAL SECURITIES MARKET ASSOCIATION.

ISSUE
The sale of a new SECURITY. An issue can be made in several ways:

- through an OFFER FOR SALE in which the issuing house buys the securities from the company and then sells them to the public;
- through a direct sale by the company itself;
- through a PRIVATE PLACEMENT with a restricted number of investors.

A company's issued SHARE capital is the face value of all the shares that it has issued. Issued capital is to be distinguished from MARKET CAPITALISATION, which is the value put upon all these issued shares by the STOCKMARKET (that is, the share price multiplied by the number of shares in issue).

JOBBER

The old name for a MARKET MAKER on the London STOCK EXCHANGE. The long-standing existence of DUAL CAPACITY meant that before BIG BANG in 1986 a jobber could not be a BROKER, and vice versa. Jobbers could only deal directly with brokers or other jobbers, not with the general investing public.

Dual capacity has now been removed and, with it, the distinction between jobbers and brokers.

JUNK BOND

Technically a BOND issued by a US company whose RATING is below investment grade, a ranking given by the two dominant CREDIT-RATING agencies in the world: Moodys and Standard & Poor's. Investment grade is important because certain large financial institutions (like pension funds) are forbidden by their statutes to invest in anything that is below investment grade. That restricts the size of the market for junk bonds.

Junk can either be high-class bonds that have fallen on hard times, or high-risk bonds that start off with a lowly rating.

KAFFIR

A general term for the shares of South African gold-mining companies.

KERB TRADING

Trading in securities outside the official opening hours of a market. For many years the AMERICAN STOCK EXCHANGE was known as the Kerb Exchange.

KRUGERRAND

A GOLD coin created and marketed by South Africa in the 1970s as a means to persuade investors to buy more gold. The original Krugerrand contained exactly 1oz of pure gold, and at its most popular (in 1978) 6m coins were sold around the world.

LANDESBANK

A German financial institution that serves as a mini-CENTRAL BANK for the savings banks of a region (*Land*). Many of them have branched out from their original function, and some have become virtually indistinguishable from mainstream commercial banks.

LAUNDERING

The process of passing "dirty" money through cleaner places (like Switzerland) in order to hide it from the tax inspector, or to disguise from the police where it came from (as with drug money). Laundering is often achieved by introducing dirty money into legitimate businesses (like construction) where costs cannot always be clearly identified.

LBO

See LEVERAGED BUY-OUT.

LEAD MANAGER

A BANK which leads the organisation of a SYNDICATED LOAN or of an underwriting of securities. The lead manager does most of the donkey work in the negotiations with the borrower, and guarantees to take up the largest part of any ISSUE that is left unsold. For that it gets the biggest fee, and top billing on the TOMBSTONE.

LEASING

The hiring of capital goods or equipment by manufacturing companies in order to avoid the all-at-once cost of purchasing them. A financial institution buys the capital goods, sets the capital cost off against its taxable income and leases the goods to the manufacturer. Much of the tax benefit to the leasing institution is passed on to the lessee in the form of lower charges.

Leasing is particularly attractive when:

- the lessee has used up all its available capital allowances (because of its own heavy expenditure on capital goods);

- the lessee does not have the CASH to make a straight-out capital purchase;
- the lessee does not want to be burdened with the responsibilities of ownership.

LENDER OF LAST RESORT

The ultimate responsibility of a CENTRAL BANK is to act as lender of last resort to a nation's financial system, typically to provide banks under its charge with enough money to stop a run on any particular one of them.

All banks are illiquid, that is, the average MATURITY of their loans exceeds the average maturity of their deposits. Should all depositors demand their money back immediately and simultaneously, there is no bank that could meet their demands. They could not call in their loans fast enough.

In such a situation the lender of last resort pumps limitless amounts of money into the system until depositors are reassured that they will be repaid as and when they wish. In the single global market of the 1990s, however, many doubt whether any authority would have sufficient resources to act in this way if called upon to do so.

LETTER OF CREDIT

An arrangement with a BANK to make money available to a customer abroad. The customer's account is debited with the required amount, and the bank then instructs its relevant CORRESPONDENT BANK to make the money available wherever the customer wants it. As a security check, the bank will send its correspondent a copy of the customer's signature.

Everybody, I am confident, understands that leverage, when applied to financial matters, involves using other people's money to try to make more money than you could by using only your own.
Paul Sarnoff, *Superleverage*

LEVERAGE
See GEARING.

LEVERAGED BUY-OUT

The takeover of a company in which most of the
purchase price is paid with borrowed money; that
is, loans largely secured on the assets of the company being bought. Repayment of the LOAN then
comes from the future CASH FLOW of the company.

LIABILITY MANAGEMENT

The business of managing a BANK's liabilities
(essentially its deposits). The knack is to structure
them so that their RISK, MATURITY and LIQUIDITY are
related to the shifting demand for loans (ie, assets)
in a way that optimises the institution's return.

LIBOR

See LONDON INTERBANK OFFERED RATE.

LIEN

Obtaining certain rights to property until the time
that a DEBT owed by the owner of the property has
been repaid. For as long as a lien exists on a property the owner loses the right to sell it, even
though he or she may retain legal ownership of it.

LIFE ASSURANCE

See INSURANCE.

*The highest recorded insurance payout on a
single life is the $18m paid in 1970 to Linda
Mullendore after the murder of her husband, an
Oklahoma rancher.*
Guinness Book of Records

LIFFE

See LONDON INTERNATIONAL FINANCIAL FUTURES
EXCHANGE.

LIMIT ORDER

An order from a client to a BROKER stating conditions that limit, for example, the price range
within which the broker can buy or sell a SECURITY
on the client's behalf. (See also STOP ORDER.)

LINE OF CREDIT

A loan FACILITY made available to a debtor by a creditor on condition that the debtor use it to buy goods or services from the creditor. Banks also provide customers with lines of credit to enable them to make a series of purchases which have been agreed with the BANK in advance.

LIQUIDATION

The distribution of a company's assets after it has ceased trading. The assets are divided among the company's creditors. Preferential creditors of various sorts (like the tax authorities and unpaid employees) get first priority. What is left is then divided among the rest, each according to the amount that it is owed.

LIQUIDITY

The condition (of a company or a market) which has plenty of liquid assets, that is, assets that can be quickly turned into CASH. In such a market it is easy to buy or sell (in other words to liquidate) financial instruments within a narrow (well-publicised) price range.

LISTING

The addition of a company's CAPITAL to the list of other shares and DEBT instruments that are traded on a particular STOCK EXCHANGE. The obtaining of a listing can be expensive. As a general rule, the higher the status of the exchange the more the listing costs. A listing can also involve a company in disclosing information that it would prefer to keep to itself.

LLOYD'S

A London INSURANCE market which began in the eighteenth-century coffee house of a man called Edward Lloyd. The market, which started as an association of London underwriters, has grown into a complex and unique organisation. At its centre are more than 25,000 names, wealthy folk who pledge their wealth, without limit, to underwrite insurance risks (see NAME and UNDERWRITER).

In recent years the market's considerable reputation has been tarnished by a series of scandals and heavy losses that have discouraged individuals from becoming names. Without a continuous flow of new names the market itself is in danger. To compensate for the loss of names, the market has introduced the concept of limited liability.

In its early years Lloyd's was almost exclusively involved with marine insurance, and it still produces Lloyd's Register of Shipping, the most authoritative listing of the world's merchant fleet, and of its seaworthiness. (See also LUTINE BELL.)

LOAN
A transaction in which the owner of property (usually money) allows somebody else (the borrower) to have use of that property. As part of the transaction, the borrower usually agrees to return the property after a certain period, and to pay a price for using it. In a case where the property lent is money, that price is called INTEREST.

---

*Let us all be happy and live within our means,
even if we have to borrow the money to do it with.*
Artemus Ward

LOAN STOCK
That part of a company's CAPITAL issued in the form of INTEREST-bearing long-term loans or bonds.

LONDON INTERBANK OFFERED RATE
Commonly known as LIBOR, the RATE OF INTEREST which prime banks in the EUROMARKET pay each other for interbank deposits. LIBOR is a floating rate, changing all the time.

LONDON INTERNATIONAL FINANCIAL FUTURES EXCHANGE
Commonly known as LIFFE. Housed in THE CITY of London, LIFFE first breathed in September 1982 and grew rapidly in both turnover and range of contracts. It has been challenged as Europe's premier FUTURES market by the highly successful MATIF in Paris.

LONDON STOCK EXCHANGE

For many years the London Stock Exchange was second only in size to the NEW YORK STOCK EXCHANGE, but in recent years it has been overtaken by Tokyo. It is still by far the largest exchange in Europe, however, and it has traded an increasing volume of non-UK shares.

These days all trading is done via television screens and telephones. The FLOOR (where brokers used to meet market makers and scream out their clients' orders) has been converted to other uses, and the size of the exchange's staff is dwindling.

LONGS

UK government securities with a MATURITY of more than 15 years. They are also called long-dated STOCK.

Investors are said to be long in a stock when their supply of the stock plus their commitments to buy it exceed their commitments to sell it.

LUTINE BELL

A bell salvaged in 1859 from a frigate called *Lutine* that had been lost at sea 60 years earlier. The bell hangs in the main hall of the LLOYD'S insurance market.

Its ringing is a doleful sound for the market, for it is rung every time an announcement of importance is to be made; in the old days these were mostly about the sinking of ships that were insured with Lloyd's.

M&A

See MERGERS AND ACQUISITIONS.

MAIN BANK

Big Japanese companies use many banks, but
each has one main bank. A main bank is much
closer to its corporate customer than any compa-
rable BANK would be in the USA or Europe (with
the possible exception of Germany). It has access
to more information about the company than any
other; it lends more; and it monitors the company
closely on behalf of all other lenders. (See also
CITY BANKS.)

MANAGEMENT BUY-OUT

A takeover of a company by a group of its managers or, in rare cases, by a team of managers
from outside. The managers set up a new company which buys the old one with money borrowed from banks. The banks use the assets of
the company as COLLATERAL for their LOAN.

A management buy-out (MBO) inevitably raises
a company's DEBT and reduces its EQUITY. Hence it
is often called a LEVERAGED BUY-OUT. That makes it
doubly vulnerable to an INTEREST-rate rise: first because a rise is likely to reduce sales; and second
because it increases the cost of servicing the debt.

MARCHÉ A TERME DES INSTRUMENTS FINANCIERS

Paris's successful financial FUTURES exchange, commonly known as the MATIF, established in 1986.

MARGIN ACCOUNT

An ACCOUNT which an investor holds with its
BROKER, allowing it to buy securities on CREDIT.
The investor with such an account is called upon
to pay only a certain percentage of the market
price of the securities; the rest is borrowed from
the broker.

This so-called margin trading can be dangerous.
It got highly leveraged investors into deep trouble
in the early 1990s when banks were lending up to
60% of the market value of shares that they
bought. (These were often shares of the compa-

nies that they ran.)

When the value of the shares fell, the banks would demand that some of their LOAN be repaid in order that the total outstanding be still worth less than 60% of the (reduced-in-value) shares. If the investor could not come up with the repayment, the banks would seize their SECURITY – the shares – and sell them. That invariably pushed down the price of the shares still further, starting a vicious circle that, with every turn, reduced the banks' chances of getting their money back.

MARGIN CALL

A demand for extra funds from a broker to an investor who has not paid the full price of his investment. The demand may arise because the market price of the investment has fallen, triggering a need to reduce the size of the loan granted to the investor in order to make the original purchase of the investment (see MARGIN ACCOUNT above).

MARGINAL COST

The cost that is incurred by adding one more unit of a product or service. A firm that is selling a large number of financial services (loans, insurance contracts, or securities, for example) may well be able to sell one more at virtually no extra cost beyond that of the few sheets of paper required to record the transaction.

Marginal cost is very different from average cost, which is the total cost involved in providing the service divided by the number of units sold.

MARK DOWN

To lower the price of a company's shares sharply following an announcement of bad news, or of bad results by the company.

MARKET CAPITALISATION

The market value of a company's issued SHARE capital; that is, the quoted price of its shares times the number of shares in issue.

MARKET MAKER

A dealer in securities who is prepared to buy and sell (that is, to make a market in) the securities of a particular firm or industry. (See also JOBBER.)

Fortune is like the market, where many times, if you can stay a little, the price will fall.
Francis Bacon

MATCHING

The process by which a BANK aligns its assets (its loans) with its liabilities (its deposits). This alignment takes place along three dimensions: currency; MATURITY; and geography.

A bank with perfectly matched assets and liabilities does not make much PROFIT. The banker's skill lies in judging the right degree of mismatch to maximise profit at an acceptable level of RISK.

MATIF

See MARCHE A TERME DES INSTRUMENTS FINANCIERS.

MATURITY

The date on which the PRINCIPAL of a redeemable SECURITY becomes repayable.

- **Original maturity.** The length of time from the issuing of a security or LOAN to the date of the last repayment.
- **Residual maturity.** The time left from today until the final repayment.

MAYDAY

New York's BIG BANG.

MBO

See MANAGEMENT BUY-OUT.

MERCHANT BANK

A UK BANK engaged in corporate finance, investment banking, PORTFOLIO management and a few other banking services. Unlike a CLEARING BANK it is not heavily involved in running personal bank accounts, or in issuing and clearing cheques.

Some merchant banks are the offspring of eighteenth- and nineteenth-century immigrant families – such as the Hambros, the Schroders and the Rothschilds – who founded them as financial arms of big merchant trading houses – hence "merchant" banks.

The power of these institutions in the UK is still considerable; any sizeable UK company with half an ambition employs at least one merchant bank. (See also INVESTMENT BANK.)

MERGERS AND ACQUISITIONS

Shorthand for mergers between companies and acquisitions of one company by another; also the name given to the department of an INVESTMENT BANK charged with handling them. Mergers and acquisitions (M&A) activity is more prevalent in economies with strong, egalitarian stockmarkets (like the UK and the USA) than it is in Japan or continental Europe.

The level of M&A activity is a mirror of the general state of an economy, and is determined by three things in particular.

- Confidence as to the future level of business activity.
- The RATE OF INTEREST.
- The availability of funding.

MEZZANINE

A layer of finance that falls between EQUITY and senior DEBT in terms of its priority in a payout or LIQUIDATION.

MIDDLE PRICE

A price halfway between the buy and sell prices quoted for a SECURITY. When a newspaper quotes only one price for a SHARE it is usually the middle price (or mid-price).

MIXED CREDIT

More often known by its French name, *crédit*

mixte, this is a mixture of trade finance and aid for the export of goods to developing countries. The general agreement known as the CONSENSUS lays down that the aid portion of mixed credits must not be less than 20% of the total.

> *Get money, money still*
> *And then let virtu follow,*
> *If she will.*
> Jonathan Swift

MONETARY POLICY

A government's plans of how to regulate the MONEY SUPPLY in order to further economic policy on growth, employment, INFLATION, and so on.

> *When two people meet to discuss money*
> *belonging to a third, fraud is inevitable.*
> Michael J. Comer, *Corporate Fraud*

MONEY-CENTER BANK

A large BANK in the major financial centres of the USA (New York, Chicago, Miami, Los Angeles, and so on) which acts as a CLEARING BANK for smaller banks in the region. Because of this wider role, concern about the health of money-center banks is greater than it is for other banks. When they sneeze, the USA catches cold.

MONEY MARKET

A market in which banks and other financial institutions buy and sell SHORT-TERM financial instruments such as bills and COMMERCIAL PAPER among themselves.

MONEY-MARKET FUND

A fund which gathers individuals' small savings and invests them in the MONEY MARKET. Money-market funds were particularly popular in the USA when US INTEREST-rate controls restricted the amount that banks could pay on regular deposits. The funds gave individuals a chance to circumvent the controls by giving them indirect access to (uncontrolled) money markets.

MONEY PURCHASE

A pension scheme in which the contributions are clearly defined and laid down, but the benefits are not. On the beneficiary's retirement the lump sum that has accumulated is used to buy an ANNUITY.

MONEY SUPPLY

The amount of money circulating in an economy. At its simplest this amounts to notes and coin only (generally called M0), and ranges through M1, M2 and M3 (cash plus all BANK deposits). The higher the number, the more (and longer-term) are the deposits that are included in the measure.

MORATORIUM

A period agreed between a borrower and a lender in which repayments of PRINCIPAL are allowed to lapse. Banks do not like to give moratoria on IN-TEREST payments because it forces them to do nasty things to their accounts.

MORTGAGE

The transfer of an INTEREST in real estate to some-one else as SECURITY for a LOAN. This transfer most commonly takes place between a house-buyer and the financial institution that is financing the purchase. In many countries such institutions are very specialised. In the UK they are called build-ing societies.

A second mortgage is a second loan secured on the same piece of real estate.

I can calculate the motions of the heavenly bodies, but not the madness of people.
Isaac Newton, on financial speculation

MSB

See MUTUAL SAVINGS BANK.

MUTUAL

Something that is owned and run for the mutual benefit of a group of members. These "members" may be the investors in a fund (as in MUTUAL FUND – see below) or the depositors in a bank (see MUTUAL SAVINGS BANK – below).

The word has given rise to the expression "demutualisation", which refers to the widespread change of mutual organisations into incorporated enterprises (with shareholders) – for example, the large number of Britain's (mutual) building societies that have opted for incorporation.

MUNICIPAL BOND

A long-term BOND with a COUPON that is issued in the USA by a municipality, county or state.

MUTUAL FUND

An open-end INVESTMENT TRUST that continually issues new shares as it receives new CAPITAL, and redeems the shares of owners who want to sell. The capital is invested in stocks and shares by the fund's managers, who are paid a COMMISSION for their services.

MUTUAL SAVINGS BANK

A group of US financial institutions found mostly in the east coast states of New England. A mutual savings bank (MSB) is much like a SAVINGS AND LOAN ASSOCIATION (S&L) in that its prime purpose is the provision of a safe home for retail savings. The MSBS differ from the S&LS in that they are treated like banks for regulatory purposes; and they are owned by their depositors, for their mutual benefit.

Together the MSBS and the S&LS constitute the USA's so-called THRIFT institutions.

NAME

A backer of the LLOYD'S insurance market who can demonstrate that he (or she) has a certain wealth which he is prepared to pledge to the market. Names are grouped together into syndicates, and each SYNDICATE is managed by an AGENT. The agent uses the financial backing of its names to underwrite different INSURANCE risks. The names' PROFIT is based on the NET premium income of the syndicate.

NARROW MARKET

A market in which there is only a small supply of goods or services being sold. The expression is applied particularly to financial markets (such as the STOCKMARKET) where there is a shortage, for example, of a particular company's shares on offer.

NASDAQ

See following entry.

NATIONAL ASSOCIATION OF SECURITY DEALERS' AUTOMATED QUOTATIONS

Commonly known as NASDAQ, a computerised information system that provides brokers throughout the USA with price quotations on a number of securities. It includes securities that are quoted on the NEW YORK STOCK EXCHANGE as well as some of those traded OVER-THE-COUNTER. NASDAQ is the main means of over-the-counter trading in the USA.

When the American industrialist and fraudster, Ivar Kreuger, shot himself in his Paris apartment in 1932, the news was withheld for six hours until the New York Stock Exchange had closed.

NATIONALISATION

The taking over and running of commercial companies by the state. The financial sector frequently has a high degree of nationalisation. In France and Italy, for example, many large commercial banks and INSURANCE companies are controlled by the state.

In recent years there has been a widespread political reaction against nationalisation (see PRIVATI-SATION). Nationalised industries are frequently seen as inefficient and uncompetitive.

NEARBY DELIVERY
See DELIVERY.

NEGATIVE INTEREST
A RATE OF INTEREST of less than zero, a feasible (though rare) occurrence in places like Switzerland, where there is a strong currency and low INFLATION.

NEGATIVE PLEDGE
A condition that may be attached to a debt or security pledging that no new debt can be issued subsequently which will take priority over it.

NEGOTIABLE INSTRUMENT
A FINANCIAL INSTRUMENT that can be handed from one owner to another without informing the original issuer; for example, a bank note, a BEARER BOND or a CHEQUE. A cheque may be made non-negotiable by the addition of the words "not negotiable" between two lines across the front of it.

NET
The amount remaining after relevant deductions have been made from a gross amount.

- **Net sales.** Total sales less amounts given as discounts, and amounts coming from goods returned.
- **Net profit.** Gross income less all costs (INTEREST payments, general expenses and tax).
- **Net worth.** Total assets less outstanding liabilities. A company with a negative net worth is technically insolvent, although it may still be able to carry on trading.

NET BOOK VALUE
The difference between the cost of an asset and its accumulated DEPRECIATION.

NET PRESENT VALUE

An estimation of the value today of a payment that is to be made (or received) tomorrow. The payment is discounted by an amount that takes into account the time between now and the day that the payment is due. This amount is calculated having regard to expected INTEREST rates and the degree of RISK involved in the payment.

The net present value of an investment project is the difference between the present value of the future revenues of the project, and the present value of its future costs.

NEW YORK FUTURES EXCHANGE

Commonly known as NYFE (pronounced knife), the exchange was set up in 1979 as a subsidiary of the NEW YORK STOCK EXCHANGE. Its aim was to provide east coast competition to Chicago's growing domination of FUTURES trading.

The largest single trade on the New York Stock Exchange involved the sale of 48.8m shares of Navistar International, a commercial vehicle manufacturer.

NEW YORK STOCK EXCHANGE

For years the world's biggest and most prestigious STOCK EXCHANGE, a barometer of the state of health of capitalism. All the most famous US companies are quoted on the New York Stock Exchange (NYSE). At its peak, the value of a single company on the NYSE (IBM) was greater than the value of all the shares quoted on the Australian stock exchange, at the time the sixth biggest in the world. Bonds, warrants, options and rights are traded on the NYSE alongside stocks and shares.

The exchange was first constituted under an agreement made on May 17th 1792. Called the Buttonwood Agreement, it was signed under a buttonwood (sycamore) tree. The exchange is now situated at 11 Wall Street, and is commonly known as the Big Board because of the huge board from which STOCK prices are flashed to the floor of the exchange.

NIF
See NOTE ISSUANCE FACILITY.

NIKKEI-DOW JONES AVERAGE
A leading share INDEX of the Tokyo STOCK EXCHANGE. It is an average of 225 major stocks of the Tokyo market.

NIL BASIS
A method of calculating EARNINGS PER SHARE which assumes that there is no distribution of PROFIT to shareholders, just the relevant tax payments.

NOMINAL PRICE
A quotation for a FUTURES contract during a period when no trading is actually taking place.

NOMINEE
Someone whose name is used in place of somebody else's. To ensure greater secrecy for a Swiss bank ACCOUNT, beneficiaries of the account often open it in the name of a nominee. The nominee then passes on all the INTEREST (minus his fee) to the true beneficiary, whose full details need never be known to the bank. However, an agreement between the Swiss banks says that they will always try to find out who is the true beneficiary of an account before they allow it to be opened.

NON-PERFORMING LOAN
A LOAN on which INTEREST payments are considerably overdue. US banks consider loans to be non-performing when no interest has been paid for 90 days or more. When they pass the critical 90-day threshold, the loans have to be reported as non-performing in the banks' accounts.

NOTE
A written acknowledgement of a DEBT, in two slightly different forms.

- **Paper money.** As in "pound note" and "notes and coin".
- **A type of security.** As in FLOATING-RATE NOTE and PROMISSORY NOTE.

Paper money was invented by the Chinese in AD812.

NOTE ISSUANCE FACILITY

A bank GUARANTEE that funds will be available to the issuer of SHORT-TERM promissory notes in a period before the notes have actually been issued. The guarantee usually involves the guarantor in buying any notes left unsold from the issue. Note issuance facilities (NIFS) are often rolled over from one issue of short-term notes to the next.

NUMBERED ACCOUNT

A Swiss invention designed to give depositors the last word in secrecy. In practice it is far less secret than mythology would have it. A Swiss numbered account differs from an ordinary Swiss bank ACCOUNT only in the number of people within the BANK who know the name of the account holder, usually just three or four senior executives. The rest of the staff know of the account only as a number.

NYFE

See NEW YORK FUTURES EXCHANGE.

NYSE

See NEW YORK STOCK EXCHANGE.

Odd lot

A transaction in fewer shares than is the normally permitted minimum on the market. (The minimum permitted trading unit is usually 100 shares.) The buying or selling of odd lots costs more than buying or selling in larger quantities. The difference in price is called the odd-lot differential.

OFEX

OFEX is a very small private trading facility in London run by market makers J. P. Jenkins. It began operations in October 1995 and is open only to members of the LONDON STOCK EXCHANGE. All trades are "matched", so fees are low.

Off balance sheet

Any transaction by a financial institution that does not have to appear on the institution's balance sheet; for example, a FIDUCIARY DEPOSIT. LEASING is off-balance-sheet business for the lessee, but not for the lessor.

Such transactions are particularly attractive to banks, which have to pay an additional price (in the form of extra RESERVES) for every extra cent that they put on to their balance sheet.

Off exchange

Dealing in shares that takes place unrecorded by an official stock exchange. In most developed countries, the amount of off-exchange dealing in equities is remarkably low – probably under 10%. But with the pressure to cut out middlemen (which is what stock exchanges are) the amount of off-exchange dealing can be expected to increase in future.

Offer for sale

The proposed sale of a parcel of securities at a quoted price to the general public. The sale is usually organised by a group of underwriters (see UNDERWRITER).

Offshore

Financial business denominated in foreign currencies and transacted between foreigners. London is by far the world's biggest offshore centre.

Old Lady

The Old Lady of Threadneedle Street, the affectionate nickname for the Bank of England, the UK's CENTRAL BANK. The name comes from a drawing by the eighteenth-century cartoonist James Gillray. It depicts the prime minister of the time, William Pitt the Younger, trying to pinch the Bank's GOLD from a chest which is being firmly sat upon by an old lady. The original cartoon is still in the Bank's possession.

Ombudsman

Originally an independent person appointed to hear and act upon citizens' complaints about government services. Invented in Sweden, the idea has been widely adopted. For example, groups of banks, mortgage lenders and INSURANCE companies in various countries have appointed ombudsmen to attend to the complaints of their customers.

Customers who use the ombudsman's (free) services retain their full right to take legal action should they not agree with the ombudsman's decision.

Open-end fund

See CLOSED-END FUND.

Open-market operations

Dealings by a CENTRAL BANK in the MONEY MARKET in order to adjust the amount of money and credit circulating in an economy. When a central bank sells securities it takes a CHEQUE from the banking system, and the cheque disappears into a black hole. The MONEY SUPPLY is correspondingly reduced.

Open outcry

A method of trading in commodities or securities where traders shout out their buy or sell offers on the FLOOR of the exchange. A potential buyer or seller of the COMMODITY or SECURITY also shouts out, and the two traders then get together to finalise a deal.

O

OPEN POSITION

A net long or short position in a FINANCIAL INSTRUMENT. The situation where investors have a commitment to buy (or sell) more shares than their commitment, respectively, to sell (or buy).

OPPORTUNITY COST

There are two definitions.

1 What investors lose by not putting their money into the highest-yielding asset available.
2 The maximum amount of PROFIT that could have been produced if factors of production had been put to other uses.

There is no security on this earth; there is only opportunity
Douglas Macarthur

OPTION

The right to buy or sell a specific number of securities at a specific price within a specified period of time (usually three or six months). Such a right can be bought and sold, but if it is not exercised within the specified period it expires. The purchaser of the option then loses its money.

There are a number of special exchanges set up around the world solely for the purpose of trading in options.

ORDINARY SHARE

The basic type of SHARE, with no BELLS AND WHISTLES attached other than a voting right and a DIVIDEND. Contrast with PREFERENCE SHARE.

OTC

See OVER-THE-COUNTER.

OUTSOURCING

The handing over of responsibility for the management and development of key functions of a business to an outside firm – in particular, the management and development of the business's IT systems. Although companies have "outsourced" their advertising for many years (to advertising agencies), the term was first applied widely to the handing over of IT functions.

Outsourcing is popular in the financial services industry. In particular, banks have handed over much of their cheque and card processing to others. Even the LONDON STOCK EXCHANGE leaves the management and development of its price-information systems to an outside firm.

OVERDRAFT

A credit FACILITY that allows borrowers to draw upon it (up to a limit) at their discretion. They only pay for what they use. A peculiarly European banking service, rarely found in Japan or the USA.

Overdrafts are popular because they give borrowers great flexibility, and do not compel them to borrow more money than they need. The nearest equivalent in the USA is a LOAN facility, a LINE OF CREDIT for which borrowers pay a commitment fee whether they use it or not.

The borrower is servant to the leader.
Proverbs 22:7

OVERFUNDING

There are two meanings.

1 A PENSION FUND is overfunded when it has received so many contributions that it is (actuarially) able to repay more in the future than it is contractually committed to.
2 A government is said to be overfunded when it has issued more bonds in a particular financial year than it needs to finance its DEBT.

OVERSUBSCRIBED

When the number of applications for a new ISSUE of shares exceeds the number of shares on offer, the issue is said to be oversubscribed. If there are 700 applications for 100 shares, the offer is said to be six times oversubscribed. In the wild enthusi-

O

asm for shares in the 1980s it was not uncommon for issues to be 20 or 30 times oversubscribed.

In such cases shares are often allocated in such a way that everybody who applies gets a (small) minimum amount. On top of that, allocations are made according to the size of the application.

OVER-THE-COUNTER

An open market for securities that are not listed on a regular STOCK EXCHANGE. Over-the-counter (OTC) markets enable smaller companies that cannot afford the full expense of a major market LISTING to establish a free-market price for their shares. They also provide a way for a company's founders to recoup some of their investment.

OTC markets exist solely on computer screens and over telephone lines; they have no physical trading FLOOR.

PAR

The nominal or face value of a SECURITY. In the case of stocks and shares this is almost always well below the market price of the STOCK. A security is at par when it is selling at its face value.

The highest price for a single quoted share was the $50,586 that it cost to buy one share in the Moeara Enim Petroleum Corporation on April 22nd 1992.
Guinness Book of Records

PARALLEL FINANCING

When two aid donors commit themselves to financing different parts of the same project, they co-ordinate the financing of the project between them in parallel.

PARALLEL MARKET

A market in a particular FINANCIAL INSTRUMENT that develops outside the standard channels for such a market. For example, the market in ADRS.

Money is like muck; not good except it be spread.
Francis Bacon

PARTLY PAID

Shares on which some of the CAPITAL is still uncalled; that is, shareholders have not yet been asked to pay all that is due from them. Partly-paid shares are not popular when they give an issuer the right to call for the unpaid part at its discretion.

PATHFINDER

A PROSPECTUS with a rough outline of a company's history and its prospects. A pathfinder is sent to potential investors in advance of a full prospectus, and in the hope of titillating their interest.

PAYING AGENT

A financial institution appointed by a borrower to

be responsible for paying the INTEREST and PRINCIPAL on the borrowing instrument (a BOND or a SYNDICATED LOAN) as and when it is due.

P/E RATIO
See PRICE/EARNINGS RATIO.

PENNY STOCK
A speculative SHARE whose price is less than $1 or £1, depending on the market. Such shares can record much bigger and quicker percentage gains than well-established companies with sizeable share prices and no reason for volatile change. It is not uncommon for a 50 cent penny stock to gain 10 cents (20%) in a day, but there is virtually no chance of IBM or ICI's shares yielding 20% in a day.

The danger with penny stocks is that they can just as easily lose 20% in a day as they can gain it. Notwithstanding this RISK, they have long been popular with individual shareholders looking for a flutter on the STOCKMARKET.

PENSION
A periodical payment made by a government or company in recognition of past services and/or payments.

There are two types of pension, based on the different ways of paying for them:

- The pay-as-you-go pension in which the pensions of one generation are paid for out of the earnings of the next generation.
- The funded pension, in which savings are accumulated over time and invested for the specific purpose of providing pensions to the people whose savings were accumulated. (See PENSION FUND, below.)

PENSION FUND
A fund set up by a company or other organisation to manage the savings of employees (tax advantageously), and to pay the pension benefits to which those savings entitle them. Pension funds are among the biggest investors on the STOCKMARKET,

but they have traditionally kept a low profile in the affairs of the companies whose shares they own.

> *The best investments are often those that looked dead wrong when they were made.*
>
> Anon.

PEP

Personal Equity Plan, a scheme introduced by the UK government in 1987 in order to encourage individuals to invest more in the stockmarket. A limited amount each year (currently £9,000) can be placed in the shares or bonds of EU companies, and the income and capital gain from these investments is free of tax. The investment has to be managed by someone approved for the purpose by the tax authorities. The savings on tax are therefore cut into by the PEP manager's fees.

PERFORMANCE BOND

A GUARANTEE from a BANK to an importer (often provided by the exporter's bank) that the exporter will fulfil a CONTRACT according to its terms and conditions. Performance bonds are often used in the construction industry when the buyer wants to ensure that a contractor completes a contract on time, and as promised.

Failure to perform according to the terms of the bond gives the buyer some degree of financial compensation for delay or failure to meet specifications.

PERPETUAL

Going on for ever. Thus a perpetual debenture is a debenture that never gets repaid.

PERSONAL IDENTIFICATION NUMBER

The number needed by every plastic cardholder in order to access their personal financial details through an AUTOMATED TELLER MACHINE. Individuals are requested to memorise their personal identification numbers (PINS), and not to carry them around together with the card to which they apply.

PIN

See above.

PINK SHEET

A daily publication in the USA on which are listed brokerage firms that make markets in OVER-THE-COUNTER stocks and ADRs. Pink sheets are printed on pink paper and can be obtained from practically every brokerage office.

Pink has become the colour of financial information. The FINANCIAL TIMES is published every day on pink paper, and many papers around the world publish their business and finance sections in the pink.

PIT

That area on a trading FLOOR where a specific type of FUTURES contract or SECURITY is bought and sold. Perversely, pits are raised not sunken.

PITCH

The place where a MARKET MAKER has his stall on the floor of a STOCK EXCHANGE.

PLACEMENT

A method of selling shares in which the shares are placed with a small number of large financial institutions. A placing is usually done in private, and is cheaper than an OFFER FOR SALE. (See also PRIVATE PLACEMENT.)

PLAIN VANILLA

A FINANCIAL INSTRUMENT in its most basic form with no BELLS AND WHISTLES added.

PONZI SCHEME

A classic con-trick that has been repeated many times both before and since Charles (Carlo) Ponzi gave it its name in the 1920s. The scheme begins with a crook setting up as a DEPOSIT-taking institution. The crook invites the public to place deposits with the institution, and offers them a generous RATE OF INTEREST. The interest is then paid out of new depositors' money, and the crook lives well off the old deposits.

The whole scheme collapses when there are not enough new deposits coming in to cover the interest payments due on the old ones. By that time the modern-day Ponzi hopes to be living under an alias in a hot country with few extradition laws.

> *Charles (Carlo) Ponzi promised to pay 50% interest for 45-day deposits based on a plan to arbitrage in the foreign-exchange markets. He took in some $7.9m. But he had just $60 on his premises when he was arrested in Boston in 1920.*

PORTFOLIO

A collection of financial assets belonging to a single owner. A well-diversified portfolio contains a mixture of assets, such as shares, bank deposits, GOLD and government bonds.

Many financial institutions offer management services to customers who want their portfolios to be trouble-free. The institution retains the assets and carries out tasks like the collection of dividends, and the claiming of rights or scrip issues on behalf of the customer.

POSITION

The amount of securities held (or not held) by a BROKER or an investor. Investors who own more of a particular SECURITY than they owe are long in the security; those who owe more than they own are said to be short in it. (See also OPEN POSITION.)

POST-DATE

To add a future date to a FINANCIAL INSTRUMENT (like a CHEQUE) so that the payee cannot obtain payment until that date. Banks are obliged not to clear post-dated cheques until the date indicated.

POWER OF ATTORNEY

A legally binding document that empowers one person to act on behalf of another. A power of attorney may specify that the power is for a limited range of purposes or for a limited time; or it may be given unconditionally. Use of the power of attorney is increasing with the rise in the number of elderly people no longer capable of managing their own affairs.

PRE-EMPTION RIGHTS

The right to do something before others, as in the pre-emption right of existing shareholders in a company to buy a new ISSUE of the company's shares before they are offered to the public. In another example, somebody whose property has been nationalised may have a pre-emption right to buy it back should it prove subsequently not to be needed by the state.

PREFERENCE SHARE

A SHARE carrying a fixed rate of DIVIDEND which has to be paid in full before ordinary shareholders can receive a penny. In the case of a company LIQUIDATION, preference shareholders have to be repaid before ordinary shareholders.

PREFERENTIAL CREDITOR

In a company LIQUIDATION some creditors are more equal than others, and they get paid first. Typically, preferential creditors include the tax and customs authorities, and certain of the company's more lowly paid wage-earners.

PREMIUM

There are two meanings.

1 A regular payment to an insurer for providing INSURANCE cover.
2 The amount paid over and above some calculated value. For example, the amount paid for a company over and above its MARKET CAPITALISATION, or the amount paid to an auctioneer on the purchase of antiques over and above their selling price.

PREPAYMENT

The payment of a DEBT before it becomes due. Some

loan contracts have a prepayment clause which allows them to be prepaid at any time without penalty (often the case with mortgages). With other loans prepayment may entitle the lender to charge a fee, which is known as a prepayment penalty.

PRICE/EARNINGS RATIO

The market price of a STOCK divided by its reported (or anticipated) EARNINGS PER SHARE. When divided by its reported earnings it is known as the historic price/earnings (P/E) ratio; when divided by its anticipated earnings it is known as the prospective P/E ratio. P/E ratios listed in newspapers are of the historic variety.

The P/E ratio is a measure of the number of years it will take for a SHARE purchased now to repay its purchase price to an investor if all its earnings are paid out as dividends.

The average P/E ratios on different stockmarkets vary greatly. In Tokyo, where investors are happier than elsewhere to receive their reward in the form of CAPITAL GAIN, P/E ratios tend to be high (often over 30). In Anglo-Saxon countries, where (higher) DIVIDEND payments are expected, P/E ratios tend to be lower (and in single figures).

PRIMARY DEALER

The limited number of financial institutions that are authorised to buy new government securities direct from the US (or UK) Treasury. These primary dealers are also secondary dealers in that they make markets in old government securities as well.

PRIMARY MARKET

The market in which financial instruments are sold when they are first issued; that is, the market in which the proceeds from the sale of securities go directly to the issuer of the securities. (See also SECONDARY MARKET.)

PRINCIPAL

The face value of a financial asset, such as a BOND or a LOAN; the amount that must be repaid when the asset matures.

PRINCIPAL-ONLY BOND
A BOND on which there is no payment of INTEREST due. The bond is issued at a DISCOUNT, and on MATURITY its full face value is repaid.

PRIVATE BANK
Originally a BANK owned by a limited number of partners, each of whom bears unlimited liability for the debts of the bank. Private banks of this sort were popular in secretive Switzerland.

In recent years the expression has come to refer to any bank that offers services predominantly to wealthy individuals. Most large commercial banks now have private-banking divisions.

PRIVATE PLACEMENT
The sale of a large part of a new ISSUE of shares (or of a chunk of existing shares) to a small group of investors, usually big institutions like INSURANCE companies and pension funds. The sale is private in the sense that it is not offered to the general public, and is not sold through a recognised STOCK EXCHANGE.

PRIVATISATION
The sale to the private sector, by a government, of businesses that have sometimes been bought from the private sector by the previous government.

The biggest privatisation programmes in recent years took place in eastern Europe after the collapse of communism. Particularly notable was the programme of the Treuhandanstalt, the special body set up to privatise the state enterprises of the former East Germany.

PROFIT
To an economist, profit is what is left over from an enterprise after all its bills have been paid. Profit is the entrepreneur's reward for the risks he or she takes.

To more practical accountants, profit is the difference between the revenue from sales and the total cost of producing those sales. NET profit before tax is what is left after all money costs have been deducted from sales revenue, that is, wages and salaries, rent, fuel, raw materials, INTEREST and DEPRECIATION. Gross profit is net profit before tax, and before interest and depreciation.

PROFIT AND LOSS ACCOUNT
Every company is obliged to produce regularly a BALANCE SHEET and a profit and loss account (P&L account). The P&L account shows the profit (or loss) made by the company during a particular period (usually a year). It shows the company's total sales (or turnover) and the cost of those sales. From the net sales figure is then subtracted the overhead costs in order to reach a figure for the company's net profit. In the United States the profit and loss account is called the income statement.

PROFIT-SHARING
A system that allows employees to participate in the PROFIT of the organisation that they work for. Profit-sharing schemes are designed to motivate employees without actually giving them a share in their company. These schemes often fail because workers cannot see the correlation between their own efforts and the company's profit, which seems like something that they are powerless to influence.

PROGRAMME TRADING
A type of trading in securities, where a computer makes most of the decisions; where computers are programmed to let BROKERS know when a significant event takes place.

When too many computers are programmed to suggest the same thing at the same time, a market can fluctuate violently. There is no doubt that the growth of programme trading in recent years has contributed to market volatility.

PROJECT FINANCE
A method of financing big capital projects – like the building of a dam or the digging of a mine – that depends for COLLATERAL on the expected future CASH FLOW of the project. It does not rely on guarantees from third parties.

PROMISSORY NOTE

A legally binding promise between two parties
that one will pay the other a stated amount at a
prescribed future date. Often referred to simply as
a NOTE.

PROSPECTUS

A document outlining a company's future plans,
particularly in relation to the ISSUE of new shares to
the public. In many countries the required con-
tents of a prospectus are laid down by law. Individual stock exchanges may also have their own
additional requirements. (See also SHELF REGISTRA-
TION.)

---

*In 1720 a prospectus was issued in London for "a
company for carrying on an undertaking of great
advantage, but nobody to know what it is". The
prospectus raised £2,000 at £2 a share before its
author disappeared.*

PROVISIONS

Money that a BANK sets aside out of its PROFIT to
compensate for its doubtful debts, that is, loans
which it feels might never be repaid in full. Banks
in different countries set aside more or less provisions depending on their prudence.

In general, there are two types of provisions.

- **Specific provisions.** These are set against
  specific identifiable borrowers who look
  unlikely to pay.
- **General provisions.** These are not linked
  to individual borrowers but are based on a
  hunch about what future market conditions
  might mean for borrowers who have not yet
  been identified.

PROXY

A vote delegated to somebody else (particularly at
company meetings) by the person authorised to
exercise it. Often used by shareholders who cannot attend annual general meetings. A proxy fight

occurs when one group of shareholders tries to get hold of the proxy votes of as many other shareholders as possible, in order to force its own representatives on to the board.

PUBLIC OFFER

A new ISSUE of securities that is on offer to the general public.

PUT OPTION

An OPTION that gives the right to sell a fixed number of securities at a specified price (the STRIKE PRICE) within a specified period of time.

QUOTATION

What a company gets when it becomes quoted on a recognised STOCK EXCHANGE. To obtain a quotation it has to meet certain standards laid down by the exchange. Thereafter it has to maintain prescribed levels of disclosure.

In return, the exchange makes the company's shares marketable by providing a price, and a means whereby buyers and sellers can get together.

RAMP
To push up the price of a SHARE artificially.

RANDOM WALK
A FORECASTING theory based on the premise that the past never repeats itself. The hypothesis is that all TECHNICAL ANALYSIS and predictions of future price movements based on past behaviour are worthless. Only theory that is based on the choice of random numbers is relevant.

In October 1857 US short-term interest rates stood at between 60% and 100%. In late 1992 and early 1993 one or two members of the European Exchange Rate Mechanism raised their overnight interest rates to over 100% in an attempt to keep speculators at bay.

RATE OF INTEREST
The cost of money over time. The difference between the rate of interest paid by banks to their depositors and the rate of interest that borrowers pay to banks for their loans is called the banks' turn.

Rates of interest are influenced by three main factors.

1 The rate of INFLATION, which acts as a floor. Only in very exceptional circumstances will a key interest rate fall below a nation's rate of inflation.
2 The degree of RISK run by the lender. Thus BLUE-CHIP companies will be charged a base rate plus, say, two percentage points; an entirely new electronics company will be charged several percentage points more.
3 The demand for money. After integration of the eastern part of Germany, the demand for money there increased greatly. The BUNDESBANK had a choice between printing more money in order to meet the demand, or pushing up interest rates in order to dampen the demand.

Each national financial market has its own distinctive key rate (or rates) of interest. In the USA the prime rate – the interest rate that commercial banks charge to their most creditworthy customers – is the central rate. The prime rate of major MONEY-CENTER BANKS sets the rate for the banking industry.

RATING

A classification of the quality of different financial instruments; an assessment of the chances that INTEREST and PRINCIPAL repayments will be made as and when due.

In the USA rating is dominated by two companies: Moodys and Standard & Poor's. Each uses a slightly different scale. With Standard & Poor's it ranges from AAA (triple A) to D (for DEBT that is in default); with Moodys it goes from Aaa to C. Borrowers whose debt is highly rated can borrow at lower interest rates than borrowers whose debt is not.

REALIGNMENT

When a currency that is part of the European EXCHANGE RATE MECHANISM is formally devalued or revalued, it is said to have undergone a realignment. The bands between which it can fluctuate are changed, and the currency is effectively fixed at a lower or higher exchange rate.

RECEIVABLES

Money that is owing to a company but that has not yet been received. A figure closely watched by accountants and bankers.

RECIPROCITY

The granting by A of certain privileges to B on condition that B also grants them to A. Reciprocity is a principle that has been widely applied in international finance. One nation's regulator allows foreign institutions to set up in its patch if the foreign authorities allow the regulator's institutions on to their patch.

RECYCLING

An expression used with specific reference to the

role of banks in taking surplus funds from OPEC members in 1973/74, and moving them on to places where they could be profitably absorbed. In many cases this effectively left the banks lending OPEC's money to other countries for them to buy more oil from OPEC.

RED CLAUSE

A clause typed in red on a LETTER OF CREDIT permitting an exporter to receive all the amount due on the letter of CREDIT in advance of the goods being shipped. Red clauses originated in the Australian wool trade.

RED HERRING

A preliminary PROSPECTUS filed with the SECURITIES AND EXCHANGE COMMISSION in the USA in order to test the market's reaction to a proposed new ISSUE of securities. The red herring contains a limited amount of information, including the number of shares to be issued. It excludes any indication of the price of the issue.

RED LINING

The allegedly once common practice of putting a red line around certain neighbourhoods and ghettoes, and refusing to lend to any potential borrower living within that area. If red lining is based on race or racial mix, then in most countries it is now illegal.

REDEMPTION DATE

The date on which a security can be redeemed (ie, the principal can be repaid). This is not necessarily the same as the MATURITY date. The security may have a fixed maturity but also have an option to call for payment earlier.

REDEMPTION YIELD

The total YIELD on a fixed-interest SECURITY, which includes the flat yield (the declared RATE OF INTEREST) plus the discounted present value of the future CAPITAL GAIN on the security. Thus a government BOND with a COUPON of 3%, a face value of

$100, a market price of $50 and three years to MATURITY has a current yield of 6%. Its redemption yield is 6% plus the discounted present value of the $50 that is to be gained in three years' time.

REFINANCING

Paying off existing debts with new loans (which are either cheaper, bigger, or have a longer MATURITY). As INTEREST rates fall, borrowers want to refinance fixed-rate DEBT. In some cases banks impose penalty clauses for such early repayment. (See PREPAYMENT.)

REGISTERED REPRESENTATIVE

A person in the USA who is registered with the SECURITIES AND EXCHANGE COMMISSION to give advice on what securities to buy and sell. Registered representatives pass on a client's orders to a STOCK-BROKER for them to be executed. In return they receive a percentage of the broker's COMMISSION.

REGISTERED SECURITY

A SECURITY whose owner has to be registered with its issuer. When the security changes hands, the new owner has to inform the registrar of the change.

Every company is obliged to keep a register of the owners of its shares. In it are noted the owners' names and addresses, the day they became shareholders, and the day that they ceased to be shareholders. The place where this register is kept (and where it is open to the public) is the registered office of the company. (See also BEARER SECURITY.)

REINSURANCE

The practice among INSURANCE companies of parcelling out RISK among themselves. If one company takes on a large risk – the insurance of a supertanker, for example – it might sell some of the risk on to a reinsurance company. The reinsurance company will receive some of the PREMIUM, and bear some of the cost should the tanker be damaged.

REMITTANCE

The earnings that migrant workers send from their place of work to families in their country of origin. For countries like Turkey and the Philippines, such earnings are a significant source of FOREIGN EXCHANGE.

In tax language, "remittance basis" refers to a principle used in taxing overseas income. The income is taxed as and when it is remitted to the jurisdiction of the taxing nation.

RENUNCIATION

The decision by shareholders not to take up their rights to a new issue of securities. After shareholders have renounced their rights, the rights can be sold to somebody else. (See RIGHTS ISSUE.)

REPACKAGING

Splitting a SECURITY into different bits (its INTEREST payments and PRINCIPAL repayments, for example) and selling them as separate financial instruments.

REPLACEMENT COST

The cost of replacing any asset that is wasting over time. To ensure that they have enough CAPITAL to replace old plant and equipment as and when needed, wise companies set aside some of their PROFIT every year.

REPO

See following entry.

REPURCHASE AGREEMENT

A CONTRACT between a BROKER and a company with surplus cash. The company buys securities from the broker and agrees to sell them back on a future date (a few days hence) at an agreed price. By the time the securities return to the broker it hopes to have found a long-term investor to buy them. Repurchase agreements (REPOS) are common in the USA.

RESCHEDULING

The creation of a new payment schedule for a

DEBT, done with the agreement of the borrower and the lender; that is, formally putting off until tomorrow what you cannot pay today. Rescheduling has been undertaken by very large debtors (such as Latin American nations), and by very small ones (like the impoverished customers of public utilities).

RESERVES

Surplus funds that are stored away by organisations to meet future expenditure. A company's CAPITAL and reserves belong to its shareholders. They are an amalgamation of the original capital put up by the shareholders and the reserves that have been set aside out of the company's annual earnings.

Financial institutions like banks have to maintain their reserves at a level ordained by their supervisors for they are a first line of defence against a RUN on the BANK.

Countries also maintain reserves (of GOLD and foreign currency) in order to meet future expenditure in trading, or in supporting their currency's exchange rate. These reserves are held by the CENTRAL BANK. Currencies in which central banks prefer to denominate their reserves (like the dollar and the Deutschmark) are called reserve currencies.

RESTRUCTURING

A rearrangement of an organisation's financial and capital structure. The crucial distinction between restructuring and RESCHEDULING is that the former is done voluntarily at the instigation of the organisation itself; the latter is done less-than-voluntarily at the instigation of a lender (or lenders).

RETAIL BANK

A bank whose main business is the provision of services (essentially loans and money transmission) to individuals and corporations. To be distinguished from wholesale banks (which deal mainly in financial markets) and INVESTMENT BANKS. Because of developments in information technology, retail banks are having to radically rethink the way they do business.

RETIRE

Two meanings:

- As in "retire from work": to stop work and (the implication is) to live thereafter off a PENSION.
- As in "retire a debt": to remove the obligation associated with the debt by prepayment (or other arrangements).

RETIREMENT FUND

Money set aside by a company to enable it to pay pensions that it has promised to its employees (see also PENSION FUNDS).

RETURN

A measure of the reward flowing from a business during a specified period – usually the reward as measured by the ANNUAL PROFIT. Occasionally, return (or, more particularly, "total return") is used to refer to the sum of the profit (ie, the income flow) and the capital gain to have accrued from an investment over a specified period.

In the abstract, the return says little about a company. So it is often used in a ratio which relates it to something else. For example:

- **Return on Equity (ROE).** This has become a key measure of the performance of companies in general, and of banks in particular. It relates return to the amount of SHAREHOLDERS' EQUITY that is being used to obtain that return. In capitalist systems that give pre-eminence to the role of shareholders, companies that do not focus on maximising their ROE do so at their peril.
- **Return on Assets (ROA).** This is a more general measure relating return to the total assets that are being employed to obtain that return. Since the assets in question are the sort that get valued in balance sheets (ie, fixed assets, not human assets), ROA is not always useful for comparing one company with another. For example, a service business (like consulting) will have very few

assets compared with (for example) an oil refiner. The ROA that it can obtain will be far higher than the oil refiner.

- **Return on Sales (ROS).** This is a measure of how much of each unit of sales is ending up as reward to the providers of capital. It may well be that increasing sales reduces the ROS. In which case, there will be a conflict between the interests of shareholders and those of the company's salesman who are working for sales-related commissions.

REVOLVING CREDIT

A LOAN with a peculiar condition: as soon as one bit of it is repaid, it can immediately be borrowed again. A revolving credit has an upper limit on the amount that can be borrowed, but no limit on the number of times that this limit can be reached.

In the capital markets a revolving credit FACILITY (RCF) is known as a revolver.

REVOLVING UNDERWRITING FACILITY

Commonly called a RUF, a GUARANTEE given by a group of banks to the effect that funds will be available to a borrower who is raising money via an ISSUE of securities. (See also NOTE ISSUANCE FACILITY and REVOLVING CREDIT.)

There are people who have money, and there are people who are rich.
Coco Chanel

RIGHTS ISSUE

An ISSUE of shares which gives existing shareholders the right to buy the issue at a favourable price within a specified period of time. Rights that are not exercised can usually be sold on the open market before they expire. Almost all new SHARE issues by UK quoted companies are in the form of rights issues.

RING

A group of investors acting in concert. Their aim is usually to manipulate prices to their advantage. A famous ring of recent years was the (ultimately unsuccessful) silver ring created by the Hunt family in Texas.

RISK

The chance of making a loss. Investors are rewarded for taking risks; in general, the higher the risk, the greater the reward. Investors who play safe (only buying US government bonds, for instance) are said to be risk averse.

In financial markets, risk takes several forms.

- **Exchange-rate risk.** The danger of borrowing in one currency and lending in another, or of having receipts denominated in one currency and payments in another.
- **INTEREST-rate risk.** The danger from, say, taking fixed-rate deposits and making floating-rate loans.
- **MATURITY risk.** The danger which arises when payments are due in seven days and receipts are not coming in for eight.
- **Political risk.** The danger of a change of government in the country of the borrower. This change may compel the borrower to renege on the debt, or somehow to reduce its value.
- **CREDIT risk.** The danger which arises when the ibm corporation gives credit to the ib Mediocre corporation.

The ultimate risk is not taking a risk.
James Goldsmith

RISK MANAGEMENT

The increasingly sophisticated business of managing the many different types of risk taken by a company. The process involves identifying and analysing the risks, and then deciding whether to reduce them or not. There are three possible ways of reducing risk: by insurance; by hedging; or by reducing the amount of the company's business in a particular area.

Rocket scientist

Name given to the highly-qualified mathematicians who are increasingly employed in financial markets as they become more and more computer based.

Roll-over

The extension of a LOAN beyond its original final payment date. So-called SHORT-TERM loans can get rolled over so many times that they eventually become long-term loans.

Round lot

The minimum number of shares that can be offered in order to make a trade on a STOCK EXCHANGE, typically 100 shares.

Roundtripping

When BLUE-CHIP companies borrow money from banks on OVERDRAFT, and place that money in the MONEY MARKET at a PROFIT. The process is known as roundtripping.

RUF

See REVOLVING UNDERWRITING FACILITY.

Run

As in "a run on the BANK" or "a run on the franc". The nightmare of all financial authorities, the sight of depositors stampeding to get their money out of a financial institution, or of a currency.

In both cases the run is caused by fear, either that the bank is going to go bust and will not be able to repay its depositors; or that the currency is about to be devalued. And in both cases the fear can be self-fulfilling: the bank will go bust if too many depositors want to be repaid at once; a currency will have to devalue if too many want to sell it at once.

S&L

See SAVINGS AND LOAN ASSOCIATION.

SAMURAI BOND

A yen-denominated BOND issued in Japan by a non-Japanese borrower; the Japanese version of a YANKEE BOND or a BULLDOG BOND.

SATELLITE BANKING

A way of organising a BANK'S BRANCH network so that it is clustered around a number of larger branches. Smaller branches provide a limited range of services; big and complicated business is referred to larger branches.

SAVINGS AND LOAN ASSOCIATION

The main provider of mortgages in the USA. The savings and loan associations (S&LS) lend long-term (and often at a fixed rate of interest). Their borrowing (ie, their deposits) has become more short-term as the United States has deregulated its markets, and more based on floating rates. (See RISK.)

This has put many S&LS in great difficulty. Those that have survived have progressively switched their business into floating-rate mortgages, and into the new areas of banking that the DEREGULATION has allowed.

Saving is a very fine thing. Especially when your parents have done it for you.
Winston Churchill

SAVINGS BANK

A BANK whose *raison d'être* is (or at least was) the gathering of deposits from small savers. At such a bank the withdrawal of savings on demand is limited. Traditionally, savings banks do virtually no business with industry, and provide no money transmission services.

In many countries savings banks have strong local roots, either as national banks with a regional structure, or as separate regional institutions. They are often set up as mutual institutions (whose depositors are also their shareholders), and not as limited companies.

Savings banks have spread their wings in recent years and become more like full commercial banks.

SCRIP ISSUE

A free handout of shares to a company's existing shareholders in proportion to their stake in the company; a CAPITALISATION of a company's RESERVES. Also known as a bonus issue.

There is, however, no such thing as a free SHARE. A scrip issue is little more than an accounting device; it does nothing to increase the value of the company. After it has taken place, the shareholders' equity is worth the same. It has just been divided into more pieces of paper (that is, shares).

A scrip issue is a useful way of reducing the market price of a share that is too high (and harmful to its marketability).

SDR

See SPECIAL DRAWING RIGHT.

SEAQ

See STOCK EXCHANGE AUTOMATED QUOTATIONS.

SEAT

The membership of a commodities or securities exchange, bought and sold at prices which depend on supply and demand. A seat gives its owner the right to use the trading facilities of the exchange.

SEC

See SECURITIES AND EXCHANGE COMMISSION.

SECONDARY MARKET

A market in secondhand financial instruments. When first issued, instruments like shares, bonds and certificates of deposit are sold in the PRIMARY MARKET. Much of their attraction to investors lies in the LIQUIDITY that is provided by the secondary markets in which they can be sold thereafter.

SECRECY

Financial agents have a fundamental duty not to disclose their clients' financial affairs against the clients' wishes. This duty to maintain secrecy frequently comes into conflict with legislation that gives tax authorities and other state bodies powers to search premises and accounts in their hunt for information about suspected illegal activity.

Many investors prize secrecy above all, and are prepared to pay heavily for it. Secrecy is thought to be found in its purest and strongest form in Switzerland. The Swiss claim that their secrecy laws were created to protect Jewish money from acquisitive Nazis in the 1930s. Since then they have also protected the PROFIT of American insider dealers and of Latin American drug dealers.

> *Outside Switzerland, the mere possession of a Swiss bank account, if not actually illegal, is taken as proof of a sophistication bordering on decadence.*
>
> Nicholas Faith, *The Mysterious World of Swiss Banking*

SECURED LOAN

A LOAN which provides a lender with the right to take over certain prescribed assets of a borrower should the borrower fail to repay. The assets given as SECURITY for the loan may be physical (like property or goods), or they may be documents entitling the holder to certain payments.

As a result of their secured lending, banks have ended up owning all sorts of things, from airplanes to fish 'n' chip shops.

SECURITIES AND EXCHANGE COMMISSION

A US government agency that regulates and polices trading in the shares of publicly quoted companies in the USA.

Based in Washington and established in 1934, the Securities and Exchange Commission (SEC)'s main weapon is disclosure. It compels issuers of securities in the USA to reveal much more than issuers of securities in any other country.

SECURITIES AND INVESTMENTS BOARD

A body created in the UK in 1986 as part of the rearrangement of THE CITY's regulation following BIG BANG. The Securities and Investments Board (SIB) oversees the many self-regulating bodies in the City created at more or less the same time.

One of the first announcements of the Labour government elected in May 1997 was the creation of a super SIB which would be responsible for the supervision of the banks as well as other financial institutions.

Previously banks had been the responsibility of the Bank of England. But with all financial institutions carrying out a broader range of functions the distinction had become invalid.

SECURITISATION

The increasing use by corporations of securities markets as a source of external finance, rather than banks and similar financial intermediaries.

SECURITY

There are two meanings.

1 Something of value given by a lender to a borrower to support his or her intention to repay. In the case of a MORTGAGE the security is the property that the mortgage LOAN is being used to purchase. (See also COLLATERAL.)

2 A certificate which gives its owner a SHARE in the EQUITY of a company. The term (which is usually used in the plural) normally applies to common and preferred STOCK, warrants and rights, and bonds (both INTEREST-bearing and convertible).

Nineteenth-century securities on which the borrower defaulted have become collectors' items. Collecting old securities is known as scripophily.

SELLER'S MARKET

A market in which the seller has the upper hand; where demand for securities outstrips supply, and where prices are thus expected to rise.

SEPARATE TRADING OF REGISTERED INTEREST AND PRINCIPAL OF SECURITIES

Commonly known as STRIPS, the practice of separating a BOND into its capital element (its corpus) and its coupons. The capital is then sold as a ZERO-COUPON BOND, and the coupons as an INTEREST-only SECURITY.

SERIOUS FRAUD OFFICE

A special body set up in the UK at the end of the 1980s to examine large and serious cases of suspected FRAUD. There were three main influences behind it.

- Concern that deregulated markets had made crookery easier.
- The complicated nature of large financial fraud cases and the need for a special investigative unit with specialist skills, in particular, skills in accounting.
- Fraudsters' ability to play off one authority against another. The SFO was designated to make it easier for different crime-fighting authorities to co-operate.

Despite a few successful prosecutions, the SFO has not been able to reduce by much the high cost of complicated financial cases.

SETTLEMENT DATE

The date by which deals for the buying and selling of securities must be settled; that is, the securities must be paid for by the buyer and delivered by the seller. With the growth of electronic trading, settlement dates have been coming closer and closer to the date of the original transaction.

SFO

See above.

SHADOW ACCOUNTING

A form of accounting used for internal purposes when a company is unable to ascribe accurately, for example, the credit for a particular sale. If two agents are equally involved in the sale of an insurance contract to a customer then the insurance company may add the full value of the contract to each agent's credit. For the purposes of the profit and loss account, of course, this will be double counting.

SHARE

A word used interchangeably with STOCK to denote part ownership of a company, granted in exchange for CAPITAL. Shares can be traded on a STOCK EXCHANGE.

SHAREHOLDER VALUE

The idea that all business activity should be directed at maximising the value of the shareholders' equity in the company. It is an idea that arouses strong support and equally strong antagonism. One argument against it as a guiding principle says that it has no meaning. For the average manager in his day-to-day work has no way of judging whether his individual decisions are being taken in a way that will maximise value to the company's shareholders.

If we wish to maximise the standard of living in society, managers should make all decisions so as to increase the total value [to shareholders] of their firm. All else is a chimera.
Michael Jensen and Perry Fagan

SHARE OPTION

Part of a remuneration package designed to encourage employees to stay with their employer. Share options give employees an opportunity to buy shares in the company they work for at some future date. The price at which they can buy the shares is fixed when the option is granted and is favourable at the time. But there is no guarantee that it will remain that way.

SHARE PREMIUM

The amount by which the proceeds of an ISSUE of

securities exceeds the nominal value of the issue. In the issuer's accounts the amount appears as share premium reserve.

SHELF REGISTRATION
A system in the USA that allows companies to file with the SECURITIES AND EXCHANGE COMMISSION (in one go) details of all the securities that they intend to issue within a two-year period. They can then pull issues off the shelf as and when they want them without having to wait for the SEC's time-consuming filing procedures.

Shelf registration was authorised by Rule 415 of the SEC, and off-the-shelf issues are sometimes also known as Rule 415 issues.

SHORT
Making a deal to sell securities that the seller does not yet actually possess. The seller hopes that the price of the securities will fall by the time they have to be delivered. If they do he or she can make a PROFIT on the deal.

SHORTS
Gilt-edged securities (see GILTS) that are due for repayment within five years.

SHORT-TERM
A LOAN with an original MATURITY of less than 12 months is generally considered to be short-term, but the expression is used quite loosely.

Short-termism is the name given to the widely recognised inability of Anglo-Saxon financial institutions to make genuinely long-term investments. More than their counterparts elsewhere, they are under pressure to show returns by the time of their next (quarterly) report to shareholders.

SHUNTER
A BROKER who deals on two different exchanges in a SECURITY that is quoted on both.

SIB
See SECURITIES AND INVESTMENTS BOARD.

SIGHT DEPOSIT
A DEPOSIT that can be withdrawn immediately.

SINGLE CAPACITY
The separation (once strictly observed in the UK) of market-making in securities (the job of a JOBBER) and dealing in securities (the job of a BROKER). It was rather like the distinction between retailing and wholesaling.

Single capacity was effectively abolished by BIG BANG.

SINKING FUND
An ACCOUNT into which money is paid at regular intervals in order to meet a large payment that is expected at some future date.

SMART CARD
A plastic credit card which contains some form of electronic intelligence – a microchip, for example. Information about credit facilities are stored on the chip so that the credit is used up as payments are made with the card.

SOLVENCY
The condition of an organisation whose assets are worth more than its liabilities. Solvency is not enough to ensure the financial health of an organisation. LIQUIDITY is equally important.

SOURCE OF FUNDS
Where borrowers get their money from. In the case of corporations there are two sources: internal and external. Governments also have two sources: taxation and borrowing.

SOUTH SEA BUBBLE
The INFLATION and subsequent collapse in September 1720 of the shares of the South Sea Company. These had been subjected to an extraordinary amount of ramping, SPECULATION and illegal manipulation. All subsequent STOCKMARKET regulation and securities legislation have been influenced by the events of 1720.

The South Sea Company's shares stood at 120 in November 1719, and reached a peak of 1,000 in August 1720. They had collapsed to nothing by September of the same year.

SPECIAL DRAWING RIGHT

A pseudo currency invented by the INTERNATIONAL MONETARY FUND in 1967 and designed to provide nations with an alternative reserve currency to GOLD and the dollar.

The special drawing right (SDR) was an esoteric oddity until it was simplified into a basket of five main currencies: the dollar, yen, Deutschmark, French franc and pound. The simplification resulted in wider use of the SDR; for example, a few commercial banks began to offer loans and DEPOSIT facilities denominated in SDRs.

SPECIALIST

A member of a STOCK EXCHANGE who makes a market in a number of companies' shares by buying all shares in those companies that are offered and selling all shares that are requested. In the USA a specialist is expected to buy and sell within a narrow price range in order to maintain an orderly market.

SPECULATION

The purchase of a financial asset with the aim of making a quick PROFIT by selling it shortly thereafter.

In a STOCKMARKET speculators are distinct from long-term investors who stay with companies through their ups and downs. In FOREIGN-EXCHANGE markets they are distinct from genuine traders who need foreign currency purely for the purposes of their business.

Although it has a bad name, speculation is essential to the proper functioning of any financial market.

SPOT PRICE

The price quoted for a transaction that is to be made on the spot; that is, the price for something that is to be paid for in CASH, now. A market where things are quoted at their spot price is called a spot market.

SPREAD

In general, the difference between one item and another, most frequently related to the difference between a buying price and a selling price.

- It is the difference between the rate paid for deposits and the rate received for loans.
- It is the difference between the YIELD on bonds of the same quality, but with different maturities.
- In underwriting it is the difference between the total cost of an ISSUE to the UNDERWRITER and the proceeds from selling the issue to the public.
- It is also the variety that a company has in its borrowings, or a BANK has in its loans. A good spread of maturities, for example, helps to give a smooth CASH FLOW.

SPREADSHEET

A series of rows and columns of numbers; for example, the premiums charged by an INSURANCE company tabulated against the age of the insured. Because spreadsheets can be extremely tedious to prepare – changing one number, for instance, may require changing them all – they have been early candidates for computerisation. Many software packages are designed to facilitate the speedy update of spreadsheets.

STAG

Somebody who speculates that an ISSUE of securities will be OVERSUBSCRIBED. Stags order more securities than they can afford, knowing that if an offer is oversubscribed they will get less than they asked for, but secure in the knowledge that an oversubscribed issue is almost certain to sell at a PREMIUM to the offer price as soon as trading starts on the SECONDARY MARKET.

STANDING ORDER

An instruction from a customer to a BANK to make a regular (often monthly) payment of a fixed amount to a named creditor. It is useful for making regular payments that do not change frequently.

STOCK

For almost all intents and purposes the same as a SHARE. Stock refers to the stock of CAPITAL belonging to a company, its common stock, preferred stock, and so on. Shareholders are people with a share in this stock.

STOCK-INDEX FUTURE

A FUTURES contract whose price varies in line with the movements of a stockmarket index such as the FOOTSIE or the DOW JONES INDUSTRIAL AVERAGE.

STOCKBROKER

A member of a STOCK EXCHANGE who is authorised to deal in securities. Stockbrokers charge a COMMISSION, usually related to the volume of deals involved, for their services. Hence when stockmarkets are busy and trading volumes high, brokers do well.

Stockbrokers were once proudly independent family businesses. But the great majority of them have been absorbed by large financial conglomerates. (See also REGISTERED REPRESENTATIVE.)

STOCK DIVIDEND

The payment of STOCK in lieu of a cash DIVIDEND. With a 5% stock dividend, shareholders receive five new shares for every 100 that they already own. If these are newly issued shares, the stock dividend gives shareholders nothing. It is more in the nature of a SCRIP ISSUE.

STOCK EXCHANGE

Traditionally the physical place where securities were bought and sold. Stock exchanges are often found in rather grand nineteenth-century buildings in the centre of capital cities. Nowadays, more and more dealing is done by brokers sitting in their offices and communicating via a computer screen and a telephone line. As that trend continues, stock exchanges become more like regulators' offices and less like marketplaces.

Amsterdam claims to be the oldest stock exchange in the world. It began trading in the shares of the United East India Company in 1602.

STOCK EXCHANGE AUTOMATED QUOTATIONS
Commonly known as SEAQ, an electronic trading network for UK securities which has a continuously updated database of prices and trading volumes, and a system that allows its subscribers to deal via their screens.

SEAQ International trades in non-UK securities.

STOCKMARKET
An organised market in securities. In recent years there has been great growth in stockmarkets around the world, in both developing and developed countries.

STOCK SPLIT
The issuing of free extra shares to existing shareholders according to some fixed proportion; two for three, for example. This merely makes more shares represent a fixed stake in the company. What was represented by three shares is, post-split, represented by five. (See also SCRIP ISSUE.)

STOP ORDER
An order to a STOCKBROKER to sell (or buy) shares in the future when they reach a particular specified price, called the stop price. Such an order is given by a client with the intention of protecting an existing PROFIT, or of limiting a future loss.

Suppose shares are bought at $1; they rise to $5. Everybody says sell, but the owner thinks they might rise higher. So he or she hangs on to them but gives a stop order to the broker to sell should they fall to $4, thus protecting $3 per SHARE of the gain.

STRADDLE

The purchase by a speculator of an equal number of PUT OPTIONS and CALL OPTIONS on the same underlying SECURITY. If the speculator can get a perfect match then he reduces all his RISK (and ceases to be a speculator as well).

STREET NAME

The registration of shares in the name of a BROKER, and without the real owner taking physical delivery of them. The use of a street name makes it easier subsequently to sell the securities, since they are held physically in the broker's custody. They do not have to be shipped back and forth to each new owner.

STRIKE PRICE

The price, in contracts for PUT OPTIONS and CALL OPTIONS, at which the OPTION can be exercised. Sometimes called the exercise price or basis price. (See also IN THE MONEY.)

STRIPS

See SEPARATE TRADING OF REGISTERED INTEREST AND PRINCIPAL OF SECURITIES.

SUBORDINATED

A LOAN or SECURITY with an inferior claim to repayment compared with straightforward loans and securities.

SUB-PRIME LENDING

Lending to people who find it difficult to borrow from traditional sources – such as banks – because they are perceived to be a bad risk. Sub-prime loans carry high interest rates in order to cushion the lender against the higher chance of default on the loan.

In the United States sub-prime lending is big business. Some very large financial institutions are dedicated to little else. In most other countries, however, when a bank says "no", a borrower has few other options.

SUPPLIER CREDIT
A LOAN to an importer guaranteed by the EXPORT-CREDIT agency of the country of the exporter.

SURRENDER VALUE
What is received when a fixed-term investment (like a life INSURANCE policy) is cashed in before the end of its term.

SUSPENSE ACCOUNT
A sort of dustbin ACCOUNT into which payments are shunted temporarily while in transit from one financial institution to another, or when there is doubt about their rightful destination.

SWAP
A transaction in which two parties exchange financial assets. For example, central banks have an arrangement whereby, if they need to support their currencies, one CENTRAL BANK will swap some of its own currency for a loan from another central bank, denominated in its currency.

With an INTEREST-rate swap a borrower who has raised, say, Swiss francs, swaps the interest payments on this LOAN with those of another borrower who has raised, say, US dollars. This can be to the benefit of both parties.

SWAPTION
An option to swap – ie, an option to enter into an interest-rate SWAP at some future date and at a price in some way related to current prices.

SYNDICATE
A group of institutions (often financial) that get together to carry out some project that each would not be willing to undertake on its own. A syndicate of LLOYD'S underwriters might get together to cover a particularly large INSURANCE risk; a syndicate of bankers might make a multi-million-dollar LOAN to a developing country. The legal documentation required to bind such syndicates together is invariably extensive and expensive.

SYNDICATED LOAN

A single LOAN that is shared among a large number of lenders, usually because it is too big for any one lender to take on by itself. Much of the international lending in the EUROMARKET is syndicated in this way.

T&E CARD
See TRAVEL AND ENTERTAINMENT CARD.

TAP STOCK
A UK government BOND issue which is sold in dribs and drabs, not all at once.

TAX LOSS
Any loss which a company can transfer to another accounting period and set off against PROFIT for tax purposes. The ability to carry such losses forward (and backwards against previous accounting periods' profits) differs from country to country.

TAX SHELTER
Any activity which provides a taxpayer with the opportunity to shelter otherwise taxable income from liability to tax. In certain cases charitable giving is a tax shelter. Investment in activities that are considered socially desirable (like forestry or anti-pollution devices) is also sometimes given the status of a tax shelter.

TECHNICAL ANALYSIS
The sort of number-crunching relied upon by believers in CHARTISM: the use of detailed analysis of past price movements and turnover in stock-markets as a basis for predictions about the future demand for shares. Technical analysts largely ignore the underlying business of the companies whose shares they are analysing.

TECHNICAL RALLY
A surge in SHARE (or COMMODITY) prices due to technical reasons. This may arise because analysts have spotted, for example, that a certain market INDEX has reached a level at which it tends to stay fixed. Or it may have something to do with the way the market itself operates; for example, London market prices tend to move erratically on the day before the SETTLEMENT DATE. (See also TRIPLE WITCHING HOUR.)

TENDER OFFER

A method of selling securities developed by the UK government, and now used all over the world. The seller sets a price (the tender price) at which it is prepared to sell the securities. Offers are invited, and applicants state what price they are prepared to pay; nothing below the tender price is acceptable. After a specified time the securities go to the highest bidder. Should not enough bids above the tender price be received the offer lapses. The whole ISSUE can then be withdrawn.

TERM LOAN

A LOAN granted for a pre-determined length of time, typically between two and ten years. A five-year loan is a term loan; an OVERDRAFT is not.

TERMINAL BONUS

An extra discretionary amount that may be paid by an INSURANCE company when a "with-profits" insurance policy expires, or when the policy-holder dies. A with-profits policy is one which is entitled to share in any surplus shown in a valuation of the relevant fund.

THRIFT

An institution whose primary purpose is the encouragement of thrift. A general expression for those financial institutions in the USA that have the word savings as the first or second word in their generic title, like SAVINGS AND LOAN ASSOCIATION or MUTUAL SAVINGS BANK.

TICK

The smallest incremental movement in a security's price that a market will allow. It could, for example, be one BASIS POINT.

TIME DEPOSIT

See DEPOSIT.

TIP SHEET

A publication designed for private individual shareholders which gives tips about hot stocks. The more influential tip sheets can noticeably move markets.

TOKYO STOCK EXCHANGE

The main market place for the buying and selling of Japanese stocks, and the second-biggest STOCK-MARKET in the world (after the NEW YORK STOCK EXCHANGE) in terms of its market value. In terms of the volume of shares sold per year, it exceeds even New York.

Stocks and shares have a rather different role in Japanese financial affairs than they have in Europe and the USA. Companies are not so dependent on them for CAPITAL; their bankers and their own resources are more important providers of funds. Shareholders are not fed with generous dividends; they have to rely for their reward on CAPITAL GAIN.

The Tokyo stockmarket is divided into two sections: the First Section and the Second Section. The requirements for companies to obtain a LISTING on the Second Section are less stringent than those required for the First Section. All major Japanese multinationals are listed on the First Section.

TOMBSTONE

An advertisement placed in a financial newspaper or magazine to announce the completion of a SYNDICATED LOAN or a new ISSUE of securities. It is called a tombstone because it consists of little more than a list of names and dates. The names are those of the borrower (who pays for the tombstone) and of the financial institutions which participated in the deal. They are ordered in strict seniority, the size of the typeface indicating their importance in the deal. Within the same rank participants are listed strictly alphabetically.

The more the tombstones, the less dead the market.

TONTINE

See ANNUITY.

TRANCHE

A part of a LOAN doled out by a lender to a borrower. Tranche most commonly refers to the chunks in which the INTERNATIONAL MONETARY FUND hands out its loans to member countries. Release of the next IMF tranche is dependent on a borrower achieving pre-agreed economic targets.

TRANSFERABLE CREDIT

A trade credit in which an importer opens a LETTER OF CREDIT in favour of an AGENT (or middle man) who then has it transferred to the exporter. This allows the agent to be the importer without putting up the CAPITAL necessary to fund the deal. It also enables the agent to keep the identities of the importer and exporter hidden from each other.

TRANSFER AGENT

An institution which transfers shares from one owner to another on behalf of the company that has issued them. A transfer agent also keeps a record of a company's shareholders, and this acts as a back-up to the company's own register.

TRAVEL AND ENTERTAINMENT CARD

Not quite the same as a CREDIT CARD. Travel and entertainment (T&E) cards are plastic slivers issued by the likes of American Express and Diners Club. They give the holder virtually unlimited capacity to purchase goods, but they do not give CREDIT. All bills have to be paid in full on receipt of the card company's statement at the end of each month.

T&E cards charge an annual fee to the cardholder and have a more up-market image than credit cards. They tend to be used to pay big-ticket hotel and airline bills, and are given by many corporations to their globe-trotting executives.

TRAVELLER'S CHEQUE

A clever method of payment for travellers that was invented towards the end of the nineteenth century. It relies on a double signature for security: the owner signs once when he or she buys the cheque at home, and again when it is cashed abroad. The payer only has to check that the signatures match.

The traveller's cheque has also proved useful for internal use within countries that have a poor banking system (as in parts of Africa, for example), or that are too large to have a single nationwide payments system (like the USA).

The issuers of traveller's cheques make a small charge per cheque for their services. Most of the benefit to the issuer, however, comes from the fact that cheques are bought, on average, 2–3 months before they are cashed. The issuing institution has the use of the chequeholder's money for that time, at no cost.

TREASURY BILL
A short-term instrument issued by a government, usually with a MATURITY of three months. Treasury bills are traditionally sold at a DISCOUNT, and their YIELD is a leading indicator of INTEREST-rate trends. In the UK, banks are the biggest holders of T-bills (as they are called); in the USA treasury bills are much more widely held.

TRIPLE WITCHING HOUR
The time when the expiry dates of three types of US financial instrument coincide:

- STOCK index FUTURES contracts;
- options on those contracts; and
- options on individual stocks in the INDEX.

Such simultaneity can move markets dramatically.

TRUSTEE
A person who is entrusted with property belonging to someone else. The purest form of trustee – one who has absolutely no beneficial INTEREST in the property – is called a naked trustee.

A trustee can act in many different roles.

- As the person charged with disposing of a

dead person's property according to a will.

- As the person charged with looking after the interests of a minor until he or she comes of age.
- As the person charged with looking after money donated to a charity.
- Even, as in the case of *The Economist*, a person charged with looking after the editorial integrity and independence of a newspaper or magazine.

TWO-WAY MARKET

A market which is as free for buyers as it is for sellers. With securities, a two-way market is one in which brokers are as willing to sell a SECURITY at its quoted selling price as they are to buy it at its quoted buying price.

UCITS
See following entry.

UNDERTAKINGS FOR COLLECTIVE INVESTMENTS IN TRANSFERABLE SECURITIES
Commonly known by its acronym UCITS, Eurospeak for MUTUAL FUND. The European Community has passed a special law authorising the sale of UCITS throughout the Community, believing that it is the most likely financial product to become pan-European.

UNDERWRITER
Most commonly an institution that commits itself (usually in association with a group of other institutions) to buying up the whole of a new ISSUE of securities for subsequent resale to the public, and for a fee. The difference between the price that the underwriters pay for the issue and the price at which they sell it to the public is their PROFIT, known as the underwriting SPREAD.

If the public is subsequently not too keen on the issue (or if the market suddenly turns against them), underwriters can be left nursing huge losses.

The term originated in the seventeenth century when underwriters wrote their names at the bottom of INSURANCE policies, thus guaranteeing to provide COVER according to the terms of the policy. The LLOYD'S insurance market still works with a similar system of underwriters.

UNIT TRUST
The name for a MUTUAL FUND in the UK and in a number of other English-speaking countries. A vehicle for pooling the small investments of several people into a managed fund. A unit trust differs from an INVESTMENT TRUST in that every time more money is put into a unit trust, more units (shares) are created. The only way to buy into an investment trust is to buy existing units.

Unit trusts are designed to give small investors an interest in a PORTFOLIO of investments. But unit trusts have themselves become very specialised.

So much so that the investor now has to think about investing in a portfolio of unit trusts.

UNITARY TAX
A system of taxing corporations based on a calculation of that proportion of the company's business that is done in the tax authority's jurisdiction, rather than on the (more usual) basis of the profits earned in the jurisdiction. The most notable proponent of unitary tax is the state of California.

UNIVERSAL BANK
A BANK that is able to do almost any type of financial business, from underwriting an ISSUE of securities to straight lending and DEPOSIT-taking. Universal banks are very strong in Germany and Switzerland, but banks in most countries are becoming more and more universal.

UNSECURED
Without any specific SECURITY against a borrower's assets. An unsecured lender has to wait until all secured creditors have been paid before he or she can get anything back from the LIQUIDATION of a debtor.

All people are most credulous when they are most happy.
Walter Bagehot

USE OF FUNDS
An accounting statement of the flow of funds in and out of a company during a year. In some countries such statements are legally required; in others they are voluntary. (See also SOURCE OF FUNDS.)

USURY
The charging of an exorbitant RATE OF INTEREST. Nowadays all developed countries have legislation to protect borrowers from usury.

- Most states in the USA have laws which limit

the amount of interest that can be charged. The limits vary according to the type of lender and the type of LOAN. Some federal laws allow the limits to be broken under special circumstances.

- In the UK anti-usury laws can be traced back to the time of King Henry VIII. At one stage in the nineteenth century anything over 48% a year was, *prima facie*, considered to be usurious.
- In continental Europe the concept is also embedded in law, as an evident disproportion between the power of the parties to a contract resulting in an exploitative interest rate being charged by the one on the other.

VALUE ADDED

The amount by which the value of something is increased by a specific process or service. Commonly used as the yardstick to justify a new business activity – as in "Where's the value added?".

VARIABLE RATE

A RATE OF INTEREST that varies in line with some benchmark. (See also FLOATING RATE.)

VENTURE CAPITAL

Money put up by financial institutions or wealthy individuals to back risky commercial ventures (often high-tech ones). This can either be at the beginning of the venture's life (when the money is known as start-up capital), or it can be later in its life (to rescue it, or to attempt to turn it round). For the high degree of risk involved, the investor expects a higher than average return from such ventures.

VIRTUAL ENTERPRISE

An enterprise that it is hard to kick – one with very few tangible assets. A company that transacts its business electronically and sub-contracts (see OUTSOURCING) almost anything that requires the use of fixed assets.

The expression is derived from "virtual reality", the semblance of reality that can be created by computer-originated images projected through personalised headsets. The virtual enterprise creates the semblance of a large corporation, but has control over very few resources.

Virtual enterprises are increasingly to be found in the financial-services industry where more and more customers are carrying out financial transactions via their computer screens and/or telephone lines.

VOLATILITY

Often used to refer to the size and frequency of fluctuations in the price of a SECURITY, or in a STOCKMARKET index.

The BETA coefficient is a specific measure of a

US STOCK's volatility vis-à-vis a base figure: the Standard & Poor's 500 Stock Index. It measures the variance of the stock's price relative to the variance of the INDEX. The index itself has a beta coefficient of one; any stock with a coefficient greater than one is more volatile than the market as a whole.

Banks and securities firms risk being reduced to a line or two of application code on a network.
John Reed, chairman of Citicorp

WALL STREET JOURNAL

The most successful US business newspaper, a daily that is owned by the Dow Jones company, creator of the main INDEX for the NEW YORK STOCK EXCHANGE. The *Wall Street Journal* is one of the few US papers to be truly national with a readership stretching from Miami to Seattle.

The paper has a very distinctive format; the only illustrations are thumbnail sketches of individuals. It is particularly well-known for several things.

- Its excellent front-page news digest.
- Its bizarre front-page articles, which cover stories that are outside mainstream news.
- Its unsubtle tub-thumping editorials.

The newspaper has attempted to become international. In recent years it has launched an Asian edition (the *Asian Wall Street Journal*) and the *Wall Street Journal Europe*. But the *Wall Street Journal*'s idiosyncratic style has yet to prove that it travels well.

WAREHOUSING

Disguising the purchase of shares in a company by using nominees to buy stakes. These can then act in concert to make a surprise takeover bid.

Many countries try to reduce the chances of this sort of surprise attack by regulating CONCERT PARTY behaviour and by insisting that all substantial holdings of quoted companies be declared to the public.

WARRANT

A certificate authorising the holder to buy a specified number of shares in a company at a named price, and within a specified period of time. This is similar to a RIGHTS ISSUE, except that the period of time in which a warrant can be exercised is much longer.

A warrant is also a written instruction that makes legal a payment that would otherwise be illegal.

WHITE KNIGHT

An investor who appears from out of the blue to rescue a company that is about to fall into the hands of an unwelcome suitor. In practice, white knights rarely charge out of the blue; they are more usually persuaded by a company that is subject to a takeover bid to come to its rescue.

WINDOW DRESSING

The practice of dressing up a company's accounts in order to make them look as attractive as possible. (See BALANCE SHEET and PROFIT AND LOSS ACCOUNT.) Behind window dressing lies the unappealing truth (unappealing to accountants, that is) that accounts are not unique and unchangeable. They can be enhanced by suitable concealing or revealing just as easily as a shop window.

WITHHOLDING TAX

Any tax that is withheld at source, that is, before the taxpayer has seen the income or CAPITAL to which the tax applies. Withholding taxes are frequently imposed on BOND interest and dividends, and sometimes on bank INTEREST too. They are very attractive to governments because they reduce the potential for tax evasion.

A DOUBLE TAXATION AGREEMENT between countries usually goes to some lengths to ensure that taxpayers are not charged twice on income from which tax has been withheld.

WITH RECOURSE

A BANK that discounts a BILL OF EXCHANGE for a customer may do so with recourse, that is, with the bank retaining the right to claim the amount of the bill from the customer if it is not honoured at MATURITY.

WORKING CAPITAL

What is left over from a company's paid-up CAPITAL and RESERVES after all its fixed assets have been paid for; that is, what is left for the day-to-day running of the business. Working capital bridges the gap between the time when it is decided to produce a product or service, and the time that payment is received for the first sale.

WORKOUT LOANS

An umbrella term for those loans made by a financial institution which are not being repaid strictly according to the terms of their contract. Workout loans include NON-PERFORMING LOANS, which give rise to certain regulatory requirements. But they also include loans where payments are overdue (or are not being made strictly according to the terms of their contract) but which are still considered to be current (ie, not non-performing).

WORLD BANK

The common name for the International Bank for Reconstruction and Development (IBRD), the sister organisation of the INTERNATIONAL MONETARY FUND. The World Bank has its headquarters right across the road from the IMF, on Washington's H Street.

The Bank was originally designed to help countries rebuild their economies after the second world war. Set up in 1944 as part of the Bretton Woods agreement, it provides long-term loans (usually for 15–20 years) to governments and government organisations. To fund its lending it borrows on BOND markets around the world at very fine rates.

It has two specialist sibling organisations: the International Development Association (IDA), and the International Finance Corporation (IFC).

WRITER

A person who issues an OPTION. The individual who at the end of the day has to buy or sell the asset on which the option is written, should whoever holds the option wish to exercise it.

YANKEE BOND

A BOND issued in a US capital market by a non-US borrower.

YEARLING

In the UK, a one-year SECURITY issued (usually) by a local authority.

YELLOW SHEET

A daily publication in the USA that is to bonds what the PINK SHEET is to stocks; a list of prices and of firms that are in the market for OVER-THE-COUNTER corporate bonds.

YIELD

The annual income in dividends or INTEREST from a SECURITY, expressed as a percentage of the market price of the security. Thus a BOND with a face value of $100, a COUPON of 10% and a market price of $50, has a yield of 20%.

- Earnings yield is the rate of return to shareholders if all their company's earnings were distributed as dividends.
- The yield gap is the difference between the yield on a reputable INDEX of equities and the yield on bonds, as measured by a standard gilt-edged government bond. This is usually positive since equities are more risky than bonds (and therefore higher yielding). On occasions, however, the yield on bonds is higher than on equities, and there is then said to be a reverse yield gap.

(See also INVERSE YIELD CURVE and REDEMPTION YIELD.)

If he wins he pockets it; if he loses he does not pay. That is known, people are resigned to it.
Emile Zola, *L'Argent*

YIELD TO MATURITY

The same as REDEMPTION YIELD; that yield which takes into account the PREMIUM or DISCOUNT in the purchase price of a fixed-interest SECURITY.

ZERO-COUPON BOND

A SECURITY bought and sold in the SECONDARY MARKET at a DISCOUNT to its face value because it carries no COUPON, that is, it pays no INTEREST to the bondholder. The purchaser gets its PROFIT from the gradual increase in the security's market price over time, as the market price moves towards the bond's face value, the amount repayable on MATURITY.

Zero-coupon bonds are also known as zeroes.

Part 3

APPENDIXES

1 The rating system of Standard & Poor's

Rating	Characteristics
AAA (triple A)	**Prime grade.** Triple A bonds represent the highest degree of protection of both principal and interest.
AA	**Highly secure.** The majority differ from AAA bonds only to a small degree.
A	**Upper medium grade.** Considerable investment strength but not entirely free from adverse changes in economic conditions.
BBB	**Medium grade.** Some speculative elements. Adequate asset cover and earnings but more responsive to business conditions.
BB	**Lower to medium grade.** Interest is normally earned but it is subject to ongoing uncertainty should business conditions turn unfavourable.
B	**Speculative investment.** Payment of interest cannot be assured under difficult economic conditions.
CCC–CC	**Outright speculation.** Obligations which are currently vulnerable to non-payment. Category reserved for income bonds on which interest is being paid but where a bankruptcy petition has been filed.
D	Bonds are in default of interest payments and principal is at risk.

Note: Investment grade is defined as borrowers with ratings of AAA to BBB.

2 Acronyms and abbreviations

ABA	American Bankers Association
ACH	Automated clearing house
ADB	Asian Development Bank
ADR	American depositary receipt
AIBD	Association of International Bond Dealers (see ISMA)
AMEX	American Stock Exchange
APR	Annualised percentage rate (of interest)
ARM	Adjustable rate mortgage
ASEAN	Association of South East Asian Nations
ATM	Automated teller machine
BBA	British Bankers Association
BIS	Bank for International Settlements
Buba	Bundesbank (the German central bank)
CATS	Certificate of accrual on treasury securities
CBOE	Chicago Board Options Exchange
CBOT	Chicago Board of Trade
CD	Certificate of deposit
CEDEL	Centrale de Livraison de Valeurs Mobilières
CFO	Chief financial officer
CFTC	Commodities Futures Trading Commission
CIF	Cost, insurance, freight
CME	Chicago Mercantile Exchange
CMO	Collateralised mortgage obligation
COB	Commission des Opérations de Bourse
COD	Cash on delivery
CUSIP	Committee on Uniform Securities Identification Procedures
EASDAQ	European Association of Securities Dealers Automated Quotations
EBRD	European Bank for Reconstruction and Development
Ecu	European currency unit
EFTPOS	Electronic Funds Transfer at the Point of Sale

EIB	European Investment Bank
EMI	European Monetary Institute
EMS	European Monetary System
EMU	Economic and Monetary Union
EPS	Earnings per share
ERISA	Employee Retirement Income Security Act
ERM	Exchange Rate Mechanism
ESOP	Employee stock (or share) ownership plan
Eximbank	Export-Import Bank
FDIC	Federal Deposit Insurance Corporation
FIFO	First in, first out
FIMBRA	Financial Intermediaries Managers and Brokers Regulatory Association
FOB	Free on board
Forex	Foreign exchange
FRN	Floating rate note
FT	*Financial Times*
GATT	General Agreement on Tariffs and Trade
IBF	International banking facility
IBRD	International Bank for Reconstruction and Development (the World Bank)
IMF	International Monetary Fund
IMRO	Investment Managers' Regulatory Organisation
IPO	Initial public offering
IRA	Individual retirement account
IRR	Internal rate of return
ISIN	International security identification number
ISMA	International Securities Market Association (formerly AIBD)
LBO	Leveraged buy-out
LIBOR	London Interbank Offered Rate (of interest)
LIFFE	London International Financial Futures and Options Exchange
LIFO	Last in, first out
LME	London Metal Exchange
M&A	Mergers and acquisitions
MATIF	Marché à Terme des Instruments Financiers

MBO	Management buy-out
MIRAS	Mortgage interest relief at source
MLR	Minimum lending rate
MSB	Mutual savings bank
NASDAQ	National Association of Securities Dealers Automated Quotations
NGO	Non-governmental organisation
NIF	Note issuance facility
NPV	Net present value
NYFE	New York Futures Exchange
NYSE	New York Stock Exchange
OBU	Offshore banking unit
OTC	Over-the-counter
P&L	Profit and loss account
P/E ratio	Price/earnings ratio
PIN	Personal identification number
REIT	Real Estate Investment Trust
Repo	Repurchase agreement
RICO	Racketeers Influence and Corrupt Organisations Act
ROE	Return on equity
RUF	Revolving underwriting facility
S&L	Savings and Loan Association
SAMA	Saudi Arabian Monetary Agency
SDR	Special drawing right (at the IMF)
SEAQ	Stock Exchange Automated Quotations
SEC	Securities and Exchange Commission
SFO	Serious Fraud Office
SIB	Securities and Investments Board
SRO	Self-regulating organisation
STRIPS	Separate trading of registered interest and principal of securities
SWIFT	Society for Worldwide Financial Telecommunications
T-bill	Treasury Bill
TESSA	Tax-Exempt Special Savings Account
TQM	Total quality management
TT	Telegraphic transfer
UCITS	Undertaking for Collective Investments in Transferable Securities
USM	Unlisted Securities Market
WSJ	*Wall Street Journal*

3 Average US interest rates, December 1996 (%)

Federal funds	5.29
Three-month CDs	5.44
Prime rate	8.25
Three-month treasury bills	4.91
US government bonds	
5-year	6.07
10-year	6.30
30-year	6.55
State and local government bonds	5.64

Source: Federal Reserve Bulletin.

4 US bond issues, 1996 (% of total issued by issuer)

Central government	45.0
State and local government	11.6
Financial institutions	29.5
Domestic corporations	11.2
Foreign entities	2.7

Source: Federal Reserve Bulletin.

5 US debt by type, 1996 (% of total)

Government securities	32.3
Municipal securities	6.8
Corporate and foreign bonds	15.1
Mortgages	25.4
Consumer credit	6.0
Bank loans not included elsewhere	5.2
Other loans and advances	5.3

Source: Federal Reserve Bulletin.

6 US corporate profits, 1994–95 ($bn)

	1994	1995
Profits before taxes	531.2	598.9
Profits tax liability	195.3	218.7
Profits after taxes	335.9	380.2
of which:		
dividends	211.0	227.4
retained profit	124.8	152.8

Source: US Department of Commerce.

7 External debt of major borrowers, 1995

	Total debt ($bn)	of which: to financial markets	Pop. (m)	GNP (bn)
Mexico	134.4	73.8	91.9	368.7
China	125.3	67.4	1,190.9	630.3
Thailand	116.3	95.2	58.7	129.9
South Korea	113.5	102.4	44.6	366.5
Indonesia	111.5	48.3	189.9	167.6
Brazil	111.0	73.4	159.1	536.3
India	96.4	28.3	913.6	278.8
Russia	95.4	35.1	148.4	392.5
Argentina	80.1	50.6	34.2	275.7
Turkey	67.8	38.7	60.8	149.0
Philippines	40.3	13.4	66.2	63.3
Egypt	36.7	6.3	57.6	41.0
Algeria	35.5	5.7	27.3	46.1
Israel	34.7	17.7	5.4	78.1
Pakistan	33.6	4.5	126.3	55.6

Source: OECD.

8 Debt forgiveness for heavily indebted developing countries, 1990–94

Creditor countries	$m
Australia	0
Austria	3
Belgium	41
Canada	701
Denmark	109
Finland	29
France	3,719
Germany	1,785
Ireland	0
Italy	384
Japan	687
Netherlands	322
New Zealand	0
Norway	79
Portugal	30
Spain	70
Sweden	77
Switzerland	238
UK	260
USA	2,274
Total to heavily indebted developing countries	10,808
Total to all developing countries	28,480

Sources: OECD; World Bank staff estimates.

9 The top 20 gold-producing countries, 1994–95 (tonnes)

	1994	1995
South Africa	583.9	522.4
USA	326.0	329.3
Australia	254.9	253.5
Canada	146.4	150.3
Russia	158.1	142.1
China	124.1	136.4
Indonesia	55.3	74.1
Brazil	73.4	67.4
Uzbekistan	64.4	63.6
Papua New Guinea	60.5	54.8
Ghana	44.5	52.2
Peru	39.3	51.5
Chile	43.3	48.5
Philippines	31.0	28.4
Zimbabwe	22.5	26.1
Colombia	25.5	24.1
Mexico	13.9	20.3
Venezuela	13.7	17.1
Bolivia	14.7	16.0
North Korea	14.0	14.0

Source: Gold Fields Mineral Services.

10 The top ten gold-consuming countries, 1995–96 (tonnes)

	1995	1996
India	479	508
USA	325	345
China	224	208
Saudi Arabia	193	185
Japan	288	170
Turkey	170	153
Indonesia	140	129
South Korea	131	126
Taiwan	160	123
Thailand	116	106

Source: World Gold Council.

11 Global proceeds from privatisation[a], 1995–97 ($m)

	1995	1996[b]	1997[c]
Australia	7,966	9,580	7,100
Austria	1,035	1,251	1,600
Belgium	2,681	1,221	900
Canada	3,803	1,762	2,000
Czech Republic[d]	1,205	994	700
Denmark	12	382	100
Finland[e]	363	911	100
France	4,136	5,099	5,300
Germany[f]	–	13,273	2,600
Greece[e,g]	–	529	1,500
Hungary	3,813	880	1,000
Iceland	6	–	–
Ireland[e]	157	293	–
Italy[e,h]	7,434	6,265	6,600
Japan[i]	–	6,379	8,700
Luxembourg	–	–	–
Mexico[e]	170	72	1,900
Netherlands	3,993	1,239	600
New Zealand[e]	264	1,839	–
Norway[e]	510	660	200
Portugal[e]	2,343	3,824	3,500
Poland[j]	1,516	495	3,500
South Korea	480	1,849	1,700
Spain[e]	2,215	1,877	11,500
Sweden	852	785	1,100
Switzerland	–	–	–
Turkey[e]	515	292	4,100
UK[k]	6,691	6,695	3,300
USA	–	–	–
Total OECD	52,160	68,446	69,600
of which:			
EU 15	31,915	43,648	38,700
Others	25,058	19,479	30,000
Global total	77,220	87,929	99,600

a The amounts shown are gross and do not necessarily correspond to the net amount available to the government. The figures are on a calendar year basis and may not add up to published budget figures.

b Preliminary.
c Estimates.
d The cumulative amount for 1991–93 is $2,240 million.
f Information on trade sales not available.
g 1996 OECD estimate.
h In 1996 there was also a convertible bond issue in the insurance group INA, raising $2,130 million.
i 1997 is fiscal year.
j OECD estimates; World Bank and SBC Warburg estimates for all years.
k The UK government has also sold debt in privatised companies amounting to £1,337 million in fiscal 1992/93, £1,617 million in 1994/95 and £663 million in 1996/97.

Sources: National statistics unless otherwise indicated.